GUIDO STEGEN
THOMAS FÖHL

HENRY VAN DE VELDE'S LA NOUVELLE MAISON

THE RESTORATION

HISTORY AND REBIRTH OF A MILESTONE OF MODERN ARCHITECTURE

Prefaces by Thomas Rabe
Peter De Wilde

With photographs by Florian Holzherr

PRESTEL
Munich | London | New York

Content

Preface Thomas Rabe 6

Preface Peter De Wilde, Flanders Heritage Agency 14

Henry van de Velde and his Return to Belgium as a Country-less Pusher of Boundaries 16

"The Making" and "The Maker" 32

The House after Completion 88

Biography 138

Preface

It was a fortunate coincidence: in November 2015, during a walk through Tervuren, I found myself on Albertlaan, right in front of house number 1: La Nouvelle Maison. I had known the house since childhood, as it stood close to my parents' home. Now, a 'For Sale' sign hung in front of La Nouvelle Maison. For my wife and me, the decision was made swiftly: we wanted to buy it. For two reasons: firstly, we appreciate the simple elegance of Modernism and Bauhaus as perfectly exemplified by La Nouvelle Maison. And secondly, it represents a piece of home, evoking memories of my years and our shared time in Brussels and Tervuren.

From 1968 to 1974, my family lived at Albertlaan 13. I grew up there, went to the European School in Uccle, and played in the street where Henry van de Velde designed and built his last residence, La Nouvelle Maison – although I was not aware of it at the time. Later, the family moved closer to the centre of Brussels. After completing my studies in Germany, I returned to Brussels, where I worked for the European Commission and then for a law firm. Most importantly, it was in Brussels that I met my wife. In 1992, Birgit and I were married in Sint-Jan Evangelistkerk (St. John the Evangelist Church) in Tervuren. So, we have many fond memories of Brussels and Tervuren – and now we are back, albeit not yet as often as we would like. My career took me to Germany for many years and, as CEO of Bertelsmann, around the world. My wife and I will spend much more time here and live in La Nouvelle Maison after my planned departure from Bertelsmann at the end of 2026.

We already feel at home there today, but it has been a long journey – truly eye-opening and much longer than we anticipated. At first, we had no idea how complex and time-consuming the restoration of a listed building would be, especially one where, after so many decades, the ambition was to return as far as possible to Henry van de Velde's original vision – much to the delight of our architect, but to the dismay of some of the craftspersons involved.

In 2016, we embarked on the project. Our first and most important decision was to choose the architect Guido Stegen to lead the restoration. We chose him because of his extensive experience in restoring houses from this era, and because, from the start, we got along well and quickly established a strong relationship of trust. We had countless on-site meetings and discussions: sometimes about outstanding permits from the authorities, sometimes about colour studies, and sometimes about the layout of the garden, which, since 2024, is part of the listed site of La Nouvelle Maison. As the work progressed, our desire grew to document the restoration in book form for a wider audience. Moreover, we decided to make the house accessible to the public. Our view is that La Nouvelle Maison should be a place of encounter, not only for architecture enthusiasts but also for those interested in the historical context of the house and its brilliant creator. Visitors can experience the captivating interplay between functionality and living environment that Henry van de Velde once created for himself and his family, and which to this day has nothing museum-like about it. This includes the rebuilt garden and its organic connection to the house. All of this together means that my wife and I feel a sense of joy every time we enter La Nouvelle Maison, every time we come home. I hope that, through reading, you can share this joy.

I would like to end by thanking everyone who made both the building and book project possible: first and foremost, the architect Guido Stegen, without whom the restoration would not have come to fruition; the main contractor, Renotec; Deutsche Werkstätten Hellerau; the garden architect Ann Voets; the landscape gardener Jo Groven and his team at elm landscaping; Katharina Haderer and Markus Eisen from Prestel Publishing, graphic designer Justus Oehler from Pentagram, and my dear Bertelsmann colleagues, Karin Schlautmann, Helen Müller, and Silke Tilk.

Thomas Rabe
Owner of La Nouvelle Maison, 2025

La Nouvelle Maison on 29 November 2015

Preface

As Administrator General of the Flanders Heritage Agency, I am delighted by the restoration of La Nouvelle Maison. It is a pleasure to see so much enthusiasm for the ingenious design of architect and artist Henry van de Velde, whose work embodies unparalleled craftsmanship. I am pleased because, before the restoration, ample time was taken to research how this unique monument could be optimally restored. Moreover, I appreciate the fact that the choice was made to stay as true as possible to the spirit and inspiration of van de Velde, taking into account the fact that the house is a holistic work of art, with the garden as an integral element.

I am pleased because less conventional paths were also taken and new insights were acquired. Finally, it is wonderful to see how this restoration project serves as a testament to the power of collaboration between owner, architect, and government, resulting in an extraordinary outcome. I offer my deepest thanks to all those who contributed to this achievement, especially owner Thomas Rabe, whose trust and vision allowed restoration architect Guido Stegen the freedom to carry out this inspiring and exceptional restoration.

An extensive and critical research phase preceded the restoration and is part of Stegen's knowledge-driven approach to restoration. Every intervention was reduced to the bare essentials. No joint was replaced unnecessarily, the metal joinery was preserved as much as possible, and concrete was repaired instead of replaced. Van de Velde and his contemporaries had extensive knowledge of living comfort. Its design, orientation, use of materials, and craftsmanship made La Nouvelle Maison an energy efficient and comfortable home long before the restoration. This made the preservation of original materials a top priority. Additionally, Stegen is committed to working in a carbon-neutral manner, adding and producing as few new materials as possible in his projects. With this purposeful approach, the architect shows how the heritage sector can contribute to a sustainable society.

The restoration was carried out with great attention to detail, such as the restoration of the subtle colour nuances on the walls that respond to the incidence of light. Van de Velde conceived the house to allow residents to enjoy sunlight and the view throughout the day. The natural colours from the garden were integrated into the interior of the house. By continuing to protect this historic property's surroundings, we ensure that the unity of this total concept is preserved and retained for future generations, serving as an inspiration for researchers and architects.

When I became Administrator General of the Flanders Heritage Agency in 2022, it was the perfect opportunity to reflect on the future of heritage care in Flanders and the agency's role in this: first with all employees, and later with the entire heritage sector. This process resulted in our 'Caring for Enthusiasm' (Zorgen voor Begeestering) vision for the future. Because enthusiasm is the fuel for heritage care, and as an agency, we want to be the anchor point and driving force for that enthusiasm. Enthusiasm for our heritage is essential: passion is vital in enabling us to pass on our heritage to the next generation. The restoration of La Nouvelle Maison and the redevelopment and restoration of the garden is one of those beautiful examples that will inspire many people in the heritage sector and beyond. La Nouvelle Maison is an icon of modernism, which we are very proud of in Flanders. It has already inspired many architects, and thanks to this beautiful restoration, it will continue to do so in the future.

Peter De Wilde
Administrator General, Flanders Heritage Agency

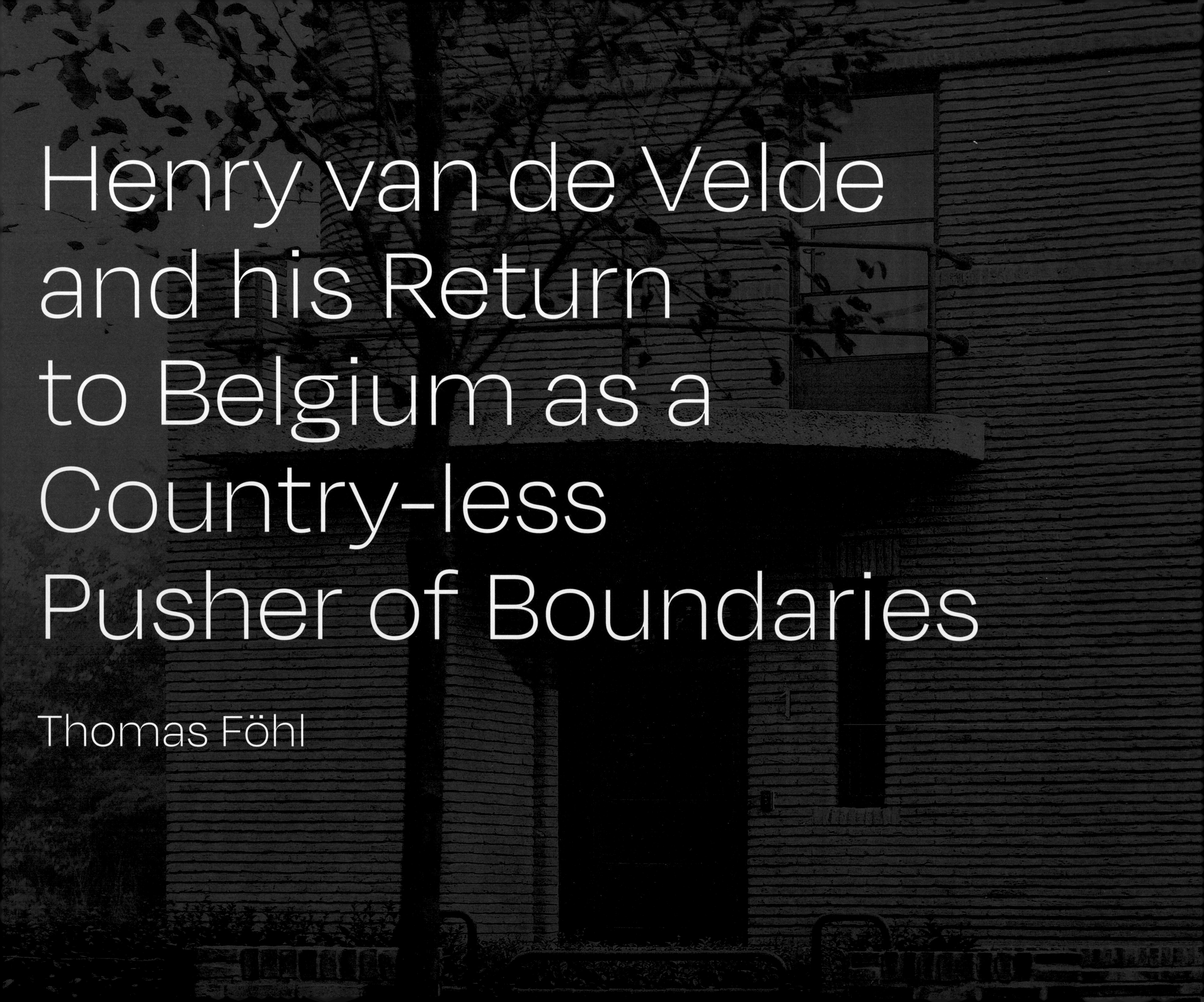

Henry van de Velde and his Return to Belgium as a Country-less Pusher of Boundaries

Thomas Föhl

'The house' is a true goal for us, and as long as we do not have it, we will feel like exiles.[1]

In the summer of 1906, Maria van de Velde reiterated this fervent wish in a letter to her husband, who was then seeking respite from the overwhelming controversies he was facing in Weimar. He found it at the tranquil Schwarzburg, a stately residence in 'duodecimo' format nestled deep in the Thuringian Forest. His impresario and ally, Harry Graf Kessler (1868–1937), had recently resigned from his responsibilities in Weimar, leaving the artist feeling both powerless and abandoned.

It was this art-loving count and ardent admirer of Friedrich Nietzsche (1844–1900) who, from the end of 1900, had devoted all his energy and extensive connections to help create a New Weimar as a beacon of modernism in Germany's geographical centre – with Henry van de Velde as a prominent artist celebrated throughout Europe at its heart and the count's hero Nietzsche, who had died in Weimar shortly before, serving as a spiritual and intellectual background. By the end of 1901, with the assistance of the philosopher's sister, Elisabeth Förster-Nietzsche (1846–1935), Kessler had successfully persuaded the young Grand Duke Wilhelm Ernst of Saxe-Weimar (1876–1923) to appoint the Belgian as his advisor. Kessler himself took over as director of the Museum für Kunst und Kunstgewerbe (Museum of Fine and Applied Arts), which became a state institution under his leadership, and then unleashed a brilliant array of activities and exhibitions. He showcased the art of the Impressionists and the Pointillists, presented modern English book art, and in 1905 organised the first monographic exhibition in Germany of the work of the painter and sculptor Paul Gauguin (1848–1903), who had died shortly before. Kessler also initiated the *Deutscher Künstlerbund* (Association of German Artists), founded at his Weimar museum in mid-December 1903, as a powerful counteraction to the pervasive German nationalist and anti-modernist artistic taste dictates of Kaiser Wilhelm II. Additionally, he acquired numerous outstanding artworks that remain treasures of the Weimar collections today. During his brief tenure, Kessler exhibited the sculptures and drawings of Auguste Rodin (1840–1917) twice, and in 1905, the Paris-based sculptor expressed his gratitude by sending Kessler a selection of watercolours for his sovereign. However, these works on paper primarily ignited the ire of his opponents due to the 'shameless depiction' of female figures. The polemics directed against him, along with personal attacks and various stories of duels, ultimately led to Kessler's resignation in July 1906. This shook van de Velde to his core, as he had co-initiated many of Kessler's exhibitions and had installed almost all of them in his museum.[2]

Nevertheless, the van de Velde family responded assertively, acting in a defiant spirit of 'now more than ever'. In the spring of 1908, the family of – by now – seven was finally able to move into their second home, the Hohe Pappeln house. Located three kilometres outside the gates of Classical Weimar and separated from the suburb of Ehringsdorf by Belvederer Allee, this secluded house was nestled amidst sprawling fields and groves in what was then still open countryside. Unpretentious yet unconventional in design, every detail of this new haven reflected a long pent-up longing for safety and protection from hostility. Developed from the inside out based on the family's needs, the vestibule became, much like in the Bloemenwerf house from 1895, the heart of an intimate domestic atmosphere devoid of any stately ambition. The first two houses share numerous design similarities, featuring complex outlines and dominant roof shapes.

The Belgian artist's houses succinctly illustrate the four defining stages of his life and oeuvre, as well as his evolving status – except for the third house, De Tent, which, as its name and the fact that it was a wood-based house prefabricated in Silesia suggest, was merely an interim home during the few years he lived in Holland.

[1] Maria to Henry van de Velde, Weimar, 16 July 1906; the original letter, in French, in the van de Velde estate, Bibliothèque royale de Belgique, Archives et musée de la litterature belgique, Brussels (hereafter BRB, AML), FSX 786.

[2] For a more in-depth discussion of these developments, see Thomas Föhl, 'Kunstpolitik und Lebensentwurf. Das Neue Weimar im Spiegel der Beziehungen zwischen Henry van de Velde und Harry Graf Kessler', in *Aufstieg und Fall der Moderne*, ed. Rolf Bothe and Thomas Föhl, exh. cat. Kunstsammlungen zu Weimar (Ostfildern-Ruit: Hatje Cantz, 1999), pp. 60–126.

House Hohe Pappeln, 1907/08

House Bloemenwerf, 1895/96

right: De Tent, 1920/21

In 1895, the radical originality of his first house, Bloemenwerf, in the Brussels suburb of Uccle had brought Henry van de Velde sudden fame. For a fledgling architect, he had created an astonishing work, although the street-facing side still presents a traditionally symmetrical configuration with a central entrance. The inner structure, however, feels somewhat disjointed, as the rooms appear to have been inserted later into the sculpturally conceived body of the intricate building. In contrast, the similarly polygonal structure of the second house's interior, Hohe Pappeln, demonstrates a remarkable maturity and confidence.

Three years earlier, in 1892, the artist had abandoned his increasingly successful career as a painter of Neo-Impressionist paintings influenced by Georges Seurat (1859–1891) and Vincent van Gogh (1853–1890) to pursue a wholly uncertain path as a beginner typographer, book illustrator, artisan, designer and, ultimately, an 'all-round artist for all'. Despite having no formal training beyond painting and the basics of graphic techniques, his universal talent – and indeed his genius – flourished in a remarkably short time. This was accompanied by lifelong writing and publishing activities of remarkable breadth for an artist, which alone would ensure van de Velde's enduring significance in modernism to this day.[3]

His 'apostolate' (as he often referred to it) or persistent fight for a New Style, a universal renewal of all living conditions characterised by reason, beauty, and art, rendered him perpetually vulnerable, yet at the same time revealed his keen intellectual abilities. What sustained him until the very end were the various strokes of good fortune in his life, as he could always rely on allies, friends, clients, and supporters who enthusiastically backed his cause, patronised him and, above all, provided financial assistance when needed.

The first of these many 'strokes of good fortune' was his first encounter with his future wife, Maria Sèthe (born 1 September 1867 in Paris), whom he met on 3 April 1893 – his 30th birthday – in Cadzand on the North Belgian coast. At the time, she was a student of his friend, the painter Théo van Rysselberghe (1862–1926). Until her death on 27 July 1943 at La Nouvelle Maison in Tervuren, she stood by him through all the ups and downs of half a century. To Eberhard von Bodenhausen (1868–1918), a long-time friend, patron, and German client since as early as 1897, she was:

> ***(…) a truly impressive woman. Her capabilities put any hardworking man to shame. And she is always above things, whether she is laughing, discussing Baudelaire, arguing that she has been robbed of 100 francs, or ordering manure for her garden. Every evening, she sits over her books for hours, trying to reconcile revenue with expenditure. Meanwhile, the house exudes an air of grandeur, and her expression mirrors that of the women in [the work of Max] Klinger – particularly her heroic mouth. Although she may not produce tangible work, van de Velde would be nothing without her.***[4]

However, this last sentence is only partially true, as Maria Sèthe undoubtedly contributed to her husband's oeuvre for decades. A talented pianist *and* draughtswoman, she actively helped him with his early designs for wallpapers, fabrics, and jewellery. She also provided invaluable advice on his typographic work over the years. Fluent in German, French, English, and Flemish, she translated and edited many of his texts. Additionally, she was directly involved in designing his clothes, even though her husband made a whimsical remark on this to Harry Graf Kessler in July 1900:

> ***Van de Velde showed me plans of houses that he was building. When I inquired about the process, he confidently stated that architecture was quite easy and merely required some basic knowledge. He mentioned that even a trained architect could have the calculations for force and resistance handled by the office. In relation to his recent forays into clothing design, he remarked that he would prefer to build ten houses rather than create a single dress.***[5]

Maria van de Velde's spiritedness was also instrumental in advancing her husband's career, complemented by her commercial acumen as the daughter of a German-born textile industrialist – a talent already noted by Bodenhausen. Nevertheless, the family was plagued by lifelong financial worries stemming from an increasingly lavish lifestyle. Maria's insistence

[3] The bibliography of his books, brochures, essays, newspaper articles and printed lectures lists more than 270 items.

[4] Eberhard Freiherr von Bodenhausen-Degener to his wife, Dorothea (Dora), née Countess von Degenfeld-Schonburg, Brussels, 12 November 1898, Bodenhausen estate, Deutsches Literaturarchiv, Marbach am Neckar (hereinafter referred to as DLA).

[5] Harry Graf Kessler, *Das Tagebuch*, 3rd vol., ed. Carina Schäfer and Gabriele Biedermann (Stuttgart: Klett, 2004), entry Brussels, 19 July 1900, p. 308.

that clients, government agencies, publishers, and Parisian art dealers settle outstanding fees and commission payments is well-documented in countless letters to her husband and to the couple's friends and patrons. Financial matters thus became a recurring theme from the very start of their marriage. High debts owed to her mother Louise Sèthe (1847–1923), who had pre-financed the Bloemenwerf house, were frequently discussed in letters exchanged between Maria and Henry van de Velde until 1915, when they finally managed to sell the house to a Brussels art dealer after years of struggle.

Henry van de Velde's inability to accurately gauge the steadily increasing flow of commissions from Belgium and, increasingly, Germany from 1897 onwards, and especially to realise them efficiently, ultimately prompted his relocation to Berlin in October 1900. For months, he had fought tooth and nail against this move, pressured gently by Eberhard von Bodenhausen, who was himself struggling in his career. It was Bodenhausen who had provided the necessary funds – sourced primarily from his German clients – for a 'Henry van de Velde GmbH' from 1898; who negotiated contracts on his behalf with new partners to produce lamps and bronze works; who arranged important, high-profile commissions for him and created opportunities to exhibit his work prominently in Germany. Yet in the end, he could only watch with fatalistic resignation and increasing helplessness as van de Velde's chaotic management and poorly qualified staff in Brussels swiftly depleted the substantial operating capital.[6]

However, the relocation to Berlin in autumn 1900 and the appointment in Weimar as advisor to the Grand Duke on 1 April 1902 marked the beginning of the most successful phase of van de Velde's career – despite numerous quarrels. It is no coincidence that he devoted more than half of his autobiography to this less-than-twenty-year period.[7]

After living in the Bloemenwerf house for just five years, the van de Velde family spent nearly a decade at the Hohe Pappeln house in Weimar, until it needed to be sold in 1919, long after the family had moved to Switzerland. The De Tent house served as the family home for barely five years starting in 1921. However, they resided in La Nouvelle Maison, their last home, from 1928 to 1947 – marking the longest time spent in any of the four self-designed houses, even though during the latter years Henry van de Velde, a widower following the death of his wife in 1943, had to settle for the lonely and demanding company of his daughter Cornelie (Nele) van de Velde (1897–1965), who had struggled with mental instability since childhood, and an ever dwindling number of visitors.

When Henry van de Velde and his wife returned to Brussels in July 1926, their circumstances were just as precarious as they had been when the 'Henry van de Velde GmbH' went bankrupt in the summer of 1900. The 1906 conflict in Weimar, which had led to the construction of the Hohe Pappeln house, also proved to be in every way comparable as a constellation in Brussels twenty years later. After having been appointed Professor of Architectural History at the University of Ghent, van de Velde had returned to Belgium in 1925 and become founding director of his new school of design, the 'Institut supérieur des Arts décoratifs' La Cambre, in Brussels. Influential friends, all prominent left-wing politicians, had worked for many years to achieve this. King Albert I and his wife Queen Elisabeth, who was the niece and godchild of Empress Elisabeth of Austria, actively supported the process. Within a very short time, however, all those involved found themselves the subjects of a dirty press campaign. Victor Horta (1861–1947), one of the great Belgian 'heroes of modernism', whom van de Velde held in high esteem throughout his life, put himself at the head of this oppositional group. The main accusation centred on van de Velde's long-standing affinity with Germany. For the time being, the artist first entered a lengthy period of convalescence, as he had done repeatedly before, at the celebrity Bellevue Clinic of his Swiss friends, the psychiatrist dynasty Binswanger, originally from Bavarian Swabia.

Except for their eldest daughter Nele, the children had by then become more or less independent. The couple, who were now getting on in years, initially resided in a flat at 200a Chaussée de Waterloo in the St. Gilles district of Brussels from November 1926, after a stint in several hotels. However, their avowed intention from the outset was to regain the needed stability of a home of their own as soon as possible. This was particularly challenging in a home country that was initially more than unwelcoming, especially as van de Velde had almost entirely forgotten Flemish, the country's second official language. This is surprising, considering he had spent most of the previous years

[6] Cf Thomas Föhl, 'Henry van de Velde und Eberhard von Bodenhausen. Wirtschaftliche Grundlagen der gemeinsamen Arbeit', in *Henry van de Velde. Ein europäischer Künstler seiner Zeit*, ed. Klaus-Jürgen Sembach and Birgit Schulte, exh. cat. Karl Ernst Osthaus-Museum, Hagen et al. (Cologne: Wienand, 1992), pp. 169–205.

[7] Henry van de Velde, *Geschichte meines Lebens*, ed. and trans. Hans Curjel (Munich/Zurich: Piper, 1962), reprint 1968. Of the approximately 450 pages of the text, which Curjel significantly condensed from the original manuscript, pp. 127–384 are devoted to the German period. For a more in-depth discussion of this period in van de Velde's career, see Thomas Föhl, *Henry van de Velde. Architekt und Designer des Jugendstils* (Weimar: Weimarer Verlagsgesellschaft, 2010, 2nd ed. 2013).

working in the Netherlands, where he obviously must have relied on German, French, and English. Consequently, he depended for years on the assistance of friends and employees to translate his lectures, essays, and other texts from French into Flemish.

Intended as a temporary solution, their brief spell in St. Gilles was to last around two years. As with all previous building projects, this delay was linked to the challenges of acquiring a suitable plot of land and securing financing for the house.

In 1926, Thea Sternheim (1883–1971), the wife of the writer and playwright Carl Sternheim (1878–1942) and from 1918 to 1920 a neighbour of the van de Velde family in the Swiss town of Uttwil on Lake Constance, provided an impressive account of Henry van de Velde's discombobulated and wounded state of mind at the time in her extensive diary:

> ***Along with Frau Schlegel and Edu Binswanger, Henri van de Velde is coming to tea. The sixty-five-year-old [sic: sixty-three-year-old] man is utterly disappointed: expelled from Holland following Kröller's bankruptcy, called to Belgium where a national smear campaign against him had begun, particularly after the royal house commissioned him to design a pavilion. To visit his married daughter [Helen von Schinckel (1899–1935)] in Mecklenburg, he travelled via Switzerland because he is afraid to reveal his family ties to Germany. 'What am I supposed to do in my old age?' he asks, aghast. 'My life has always been so precise. I am unable to adjust.' As the conversation shifts to Mallarmé, Gide and Ghéon, he visibly warms and begins to share such an in-depth account that Karl implores him to preserve these very interesting facts – most of which are no longer familiar to our generation – by writing them down for posterity. He promises to do his best to find a publisher.***[8]

A few months later, Maria van de Velde wrote a lengthy letter to her long-time Berlin friend Sophie Herrmann (1872–1931), an early client of her husband who had been wearing his clothes and his jewellery since 1897. In it, Maria described the couple's situation at the time and expressed her concerns about their eldest daughter Nele, who, with brief interruptions, had been undergoing psychiatric treatment with the Binswangers since the early 1920s. Progress was painfully slow, and the ever-increasing costs of Nele's treatment in Kreuzlingen placed an enormous burden on the family:

> ***(...) but we can hardly make those sacrifices anymore, especially since Henry, while appointed, is still not in office due to the ongoing difficulties imposed by the Ministry of Finance, where his opponents are located. We have been in a state of constant anticipation for 8 months now. Henry gives a three-hour lecture in Ghent every week. He finds satisfaction in it, but the first year requires a colossal amount of work that is to be translated into Flemish. Our circle of friends here will probably be completely reconfigured. We encounter some of our old friends who have remained youthful in spirit, while others seem stagnant & show early signs of fatigue. Henry enthrals the youths & they are on the rise. Then they will be like Vandervelde, Vermeylen and others who never grow old.***[9]

Shortly afterwards, van de Velde finally found a suitable plot of land for his fourth house in the suburb of Tervuren, east of Brussels, on land belonging to the Crown Estate. This circumstance contributed to the predictable attacks against him at the time, as his return to Belgium was also linked to the king's intention for van de Velde to design an opulent villa for the royal couple in Lombardsijde in western Flanders, marking the first project of his new and deliberately programmatic engagement for Belgium. This desire became another significant issue in the press campaign against him and others involved, culminating in inflammatory headlines such as *Tout, mais pas ça* ('Everything, but not that').

According to a letter to his wife dated 9 July 1927, he had already drawn the plans for the new house, even though the building site found in Tervuren that same month was by no means a definitive purchase option yet.[10] It is important to note that Henry van de Velde had never personally drawn the construction and execution plans for his many architectural

[8] Thea Sternheim, *Tagebücher 1903–1971*, ed. Thomas Ehrsam and Regula Wyss, 5 vols. (Göttingen: Wallstein, 2002), entry Uttwil, 3 October 1926, vol. 2, p. 47. The Marie-Louise Schlegel (1871–1941) mentioned here was previously married to the Kreuzlingen psychiatrist and clinic director Dr Robert Binswanger (1850–1910). In autumn 1920, she and her brother-in-law Prof Dr Otto Binswanger (1852–1929) had bought the house on the lake in Uttwil from van de Velde, who had acquired it at the end of 1918. 'Edu' refers to Marie-Louise's son, Dr Paul Eduard Binswanger (1898–1959).

[9] Maria van de Velde to Sophie Herrmann, Brussels, 19 February 1927, Curt Herrmann estate, private collection. The 'Vandervelde' and 'Vermeylen' she mentions are the left-wing politician Émile Guillaume Vandervelde (1866–1938), who played a key role in van de Velde's appointment from 1922, and the writer, critic, politician and previously committed anarchist Auguste Vermeylen (1872–1945). Both were close friends of Henry van de Velde from the 1880s onwards. Vandervelde's second wife, the physician and left-wing politician Dr Jeanne Vandervelde (1891–1963), only joined his circle of friends at this time.

[10] Letter preserved in the van de Velde estate, Bibliothèque royale de Belgique (BRB), AML, FSX 784.

projects throughout his long career. He sketched his designs in various forms and tested spatial volumes or individual details using three-dimensional models in plaster, clay, or plasticine, but he never created self-drawn planning documents sufficient for construction. In the context of La Nouvelle Maison, it is crucial to mention the two Belgian architects and later friends Jean-Jules Eggericx (1884–1963) and Raphaël Verwilghen (1885–1963). From 1923 to 1937, the two partnered in an office, primarily focusing on urban planning projects. Jean-Jules Eggericx later taught at La Cambre as Professor of Architecture (1929–46) and subsequently as Professor of Urban Planning (1947–49). Raphaël Verwilghen, in turn, was his predecessor as Professor of Urban Planning at La Cambre from 1928 to 1946. The two architects were responsible for the technical realisation of the La Nouvelle Maison project, although it is unclear today what portion of the construction work can be attributed to each of them. After Henry van de Velde and his daughter Nele moved to Switzerland in 1947, Verwilghen became custodian of the house until 1963. Following Henry van de Velde's death, he devoted considerable effort to ensuring that his estate was returned from Zurich to Brussels. A bachelor, Verwilghen himself lived nearby in Tervuren, first with his mother, who passed away in 1938, and later with his two elderly sisters.

In autumn 1927, van de Velde was finally able to submit his plans for La Nouvelle Maison. In the Grand *manuscrit* of his autobiography, he reflected on his 1926 commission for the 'Lombardsijde' project and – closely related to this – the refusal to issue a permit for the plans he had submitted shortly before for the construction of his La Nouvelle Maison. The main adversary in this context was the Director General of the Crown Estate, he explained:

> ***His Majesty Albert I had insisted on stating in front of me and hinting to others that it would be 'me or no-one' who would build the royal villa (…). Towards the end of 1927, a document finally arrived at the king's office: the contract, drafted by the department that was undoubtedly responsible for the expenditure. A clause stated: 'the façades shall be decorated!' Was this stipulation made intentionally? I recognised [the style] of the official, the Director General of the Crown Estate, who had refused to grant permission to build my villa 'Nouvelle Maison' on the land I had acquired from his department on the pretext that 'the architecture differed too much from the neighbouring villas!' I had to oppose this decision, and the threat of submitting said refusal to the 'Society of Architects and Town Planners' made the Director General hesitate, who in the meantime had decided to inform himself, only to realise the ridicule to which he would face if informed critics, both Belgian and foreign, publicised the enormous stupidity of the reason given.***
>
> ***I shall not dwell on the bad taste (…) and lack of aesthetic culture among the newly affluent bourgeoisie. It was enough for me to sense that a foreign intervention would come between the sovereigns, who placed their trust in me, for me to fear the worst and lose all hope – before even beginning the execution of the plans – of successfully completing the project! The clause regarding 'decorated facades' spoke volumes, and I felt it necessary to keep the Sovereigns out of the inevitable disputes that would arise between the officials, no matter where they came from – and they would come from everywhere – and myself over opposing views on aesthetics.***[11]

They sought to remind him of the traditional standards of the 'nouveau riche' and insisted – much like for the royal couple's villa, which was never realised – on a decorative, conventional-style façade. However, as described, Henry van de Velde successfully resisted this demand.

La Nouvelle Maison was the first building that the artist was able to realise after returning to his home country, alongside the town house for the textile industrialist Georges Cohen (1887–1960) in Brussels, which was designed at around the same time. It also marks the beginning of the final phase of his enormous oeuvre, a period that has been insufficiently studied to date, apart from the efforts by Günther Stamm, who began focusing on this subject in 1963.[12]

[11] BRB, AML, van de Velde estate, FSX 10, published in Léon Ploegaerts, *Henry van de Velde. Les mémoires inachevés d'un artiste européen. Édition critique*, 2 vols. (Brussels: Académie royale de Belgique, 1999), here vol. 1, p. 443.

[12] Günther Stamm, *Studien zur Architektur und Architekturtheorie Henry van de Veldes*, diss. University of Göttingen, printed from a typescript, 1969. While individual buildings have meanwhile been examined, a well-founded general overview is still lacking, even after the publication of Léon Ploegaerts and Pierre Puttemans' comprehensive catalogue, *L'œuvre architecturale de Henry van de Velde* (Brussels and Quebec: Vokaer and Presse de l'Université de Laval, 1987). This essay was written in spring 2020, and since then, the third annotated volume of Henry van de Velde's autobiography was published in two half-volumes in 2023. In this publication, as in Ploegaerts 1999 (see n. 11), van de Velde's memoirs were again edited in French. The first two volumes were published as long ago as 1992 and 1995, and so the third volume was not foreseeable in 2020. See Anne van Loo, with the assistance of Fabrice van de Kerckhove, *Henry van de Velde, Récit de ma vie*, vol. 1 (1863–1900) (Brussels: Versa, 1992); Van Loo, *Henry van de Velde. Récit de ma vie*, vol. 2 (1900–17) (Brussels: Versa, 1995); Van Loo, *Henry van de Velde. Récit de ma vie*, vols. 3.1 and 3.2 (1917–57) (Turnhout: Brepols, 2023). The third volume focuses and comments on Henry van de Velde's projects and their context from the beginning of the 1920s onwards. However, many of the projects from this period still await thorough analysis.

But what had changed in the meantime, and how did the Belgian artist navigate this task in a situation that demanded everything from him one last time – now, as it were, a 'pensioner' amidst a prominent cohort of young architects belonging to a completely new generation after the upheaval of the First World War?

From 1910 onwards, the first signs of insecurity appeared in Henry van de Velde's architecture, as in many of his solutions for furniture, interior decorations, and silverware. He had worked for several upper-class and aristocratic clients in Germany and had, albeit reluctantly, bowed down to their demands for prestigious objects. While exceptions were common, the prevailing trend and a noticeable resignation were unmistakable. This tendency continued after 1920 during his activities in The Hague, where he worked for the Rotterdam-born merchant and industrialist Anton Kröller (1862–1941) and his German wife Helene Kröller-Müller (1869–1939), who had amassed, in just a few years, the largest privately owned collection of over one hundred paintings by Vincent van Gogh. Some of his plans during this period displayed a tendency towards monumental forms, which veered into megalomania in the series of designs for the Kröller-Müller Museum in Hoenderloo – a disconcerting tendency, even disregarding the fact that these plans were never realised. However, this applied to a lesser extent to purely functional buildings, where one can still recognise van de Velde's lifelong ambition to create clean lines, use appropriate materials, and insist on functionality.

After returning to Belgium in 1926, Henry van de Velde regained his composure – indeed, one might say that he almost reinvented himself once again based on the principles for which he had advocated since the 1890s. In this context, La Nouvelle Maison became the starting point for his late work. Although, at first glance, the building's emphatically stereometric forms align with the then prevailing ideas of the international 'New Objectivity' avant-garde, the artist masterfully infused his individual style, transforming the demanded purity of the primary form from the aseptic introversion of the white cube made of concrete, glass, and steel into a dynamic, sculptural, extroverted structure. He achieved this through a few simple manipulations, such as the subtle colours of the hard-fired brick veneer and its joints, the horizontal differentiation of the bricklayers, the rounded corners on all sides, the gently concave, inviting recesses at the base of the elegant studio or the finely detailed overhangs of exposed concrete on the roof and the two terraces. In this design, Henry van de Velde played with loosely proportioned cubes and ultimately created an outdoor architectural sculpture without developing a main façade or aspiring to stateliness. [13]

While the clear layout of the upper floor is strictly informed by the central axis of the corridor, the ground floor unfolds through the entrance hall and the long library gallery ('galerie-bibliothèque') into an open and spacious living area connected to the dining room, the protruding studio and the garden. This layout evokes the informal and intimate design of the Hohe Pappeln house. The early portrait of Maria Sèthe in van de Velde's workroom, commissioned from Théo van Rysselberghe in 1891 by her parents, along with the portraits of her two sisters Alice Dubois (1869–1944) and Irma Saenger-Sèthe (1876–1958) hanging nearby, also became an important reference point for the main axis. The large-scale painting had previously dictated the colour scheme of the walls and fixtures in the hall of the Bloemenwerf house, with the dominant violet of Maria's dress and the curtain of the same colour in the background, complemented by the yellow of her hair and the honey-coloured tones of the chair and harmonium. The reference to the subtlety of pointillist colour application, characterised by countless individual dabs of paint was now apparent again in La Nouvelle Maison, albeit in a more understated and less bold manner. The skills of a great artist-architect who began his career as a painter were once again clearly on display here.

The Swabian architect Hugo Häring (1882–1958), who, in his youth, was an enthusiastic admirer of Henry van de Velde and later himself a prominent modernist who sadly receives far too little attention today, maintained a cordial relationship with the Belgian architect in the 1920s and 1930s. Reflecting on his own work in 1952, Häring aptly and lucidly characterised Henry van de Velde's design process, a description that resonates with the designs of both Hohe Pappeln and La Nouvelle Maison:

[13] See Guido Stegen's essay on the significance of the materiality of the exposed concrete and the brick veneer, its colouring and jointing. The same high quality found in La Nouvelle Maison is evident in most of the buildings he designed during that period and later in Belgium and Germany.

Théo van Rysselberghe,
Maria Sèthe at the Harmonium, 1891

View from the south-west

View from the south-east

The construction site, 1928

The completed building, 1929

It is a matter of laying out the house from the inside outwards, starting with the active processes of dwelling (…). The exterior is no longer determined in advance (…) it does not dictate its form. One builds walls around dwelling clusters, rather than forcing dwelling clusters into rectangles. Working this way, walls are unlikely to end up at right angles, nor is one likely to create a rectangular building. (…) A natural order will assert itself, with each part finding its appropriate relation to the sun, allowing the house to extend radially towards the south and from east to west, while turning its back to the north. It behaves like a plant presenting its organs to the sun.[14]

When furnishing La Nouvelle Maison, Henry van de Velde reused much of the furniture that had served him well in previous houses and flats in Brussels, Berlin, Weimar, and Holland. Some pieces were refurbished, repainted, or upholstered with fresh fabrics, and the only additions were the chest-high bookcases in the library gallery, large built-in wardrobes on the upper floor, and some modern furniture designed by his colleagues and friends Huib Hoste (1881–1957) and Alvar Aalto (1898–1976). Assisting him in this endeavour was his pupil at the time, Nicolaus (Nic) Schubert (1906–2001) from Uttwil, Switzerland. Schubert was a trained cabinetmaker who additionally obtained a degree in interior design at La Cambre and remained in Brussels until 1931, before later taking over his father's furniture factory, Schubert & Schramm, in his hometown on Lake Constance.[15] Today, the movable furniture is scattered across museums worldwide. For instance, the early dining room from the Bloemenwerf house is in the ZAZ Bellerive in Zurich, while other individual pieces of furniture can be found in Ghent, Weimar, private collections, and Japan. Unfortunately, some of the furniture is considered lost. In some areas, inexpensive seamed seagrass mats from Java were used as floor coverings, a practice common in many interiors since around 1897. Overall, the interior decoration once again reflects, much like the construction of the Hohe Pappeln house, the necessity to keep overall costs in check. However, the decision to reuse old furniture was likely also influenced by sentimental attachments. Additionally, parts of the collection had to be sold in 1928–29 to finance the house. One of the divested works was the painting *Le Pont* by Georges Seurat (1882–83), which was sold in 1929 through Galerie Bernheim-Jeune in Paris and is now housed in the Metropolitan Museum of Art in New York. This painting was one of van de Velde's favourites, and he had owned it for over forty years.

Until the late 1930s, numerous surviving private photographs capture the bustling life within the house, filled with children, spouses, grandchildren, and friends. The many bedrooms proved useful for accommodating this lively household. Initially, it was also planned that the youngest children, the twins Thylla and Thyl, born in Weimar in 1904, would live there; however, both married nearly simultaneously, in December 1929 and January 1930, respectively.

In the Netherlands until 1925, the van de Velde family had still frequently welcomed visitors from Germany – old friends and former clients, journalists and other protagonists of modernism interested in Henry van de Velde's art. However, after their return to Belgium, this flow of visitors slowed and shifted to the exchange of letters. An exception was Harry Graf Kessler, who unexpectedly showed up in Brussels on 19 May 1930 where he and Henry van de Velde met in person for the last time. As Kessler noted in his diary:

In the morning with Vandevelde at his institute in the Abbaye de la Cambre, an old monastery that the government had made available for his school. He gave us a tour, showing us the various departments (16 professors), the print shop, the theatre school and so on. There were many foreign students, including a Polish woman and a Romanian woman, among others (…) – In the evening I dined at Vandevelde's new house in Tervueren. The house is quite lovely, showing some influence from Le Corbusier, yet built in the true Vandevelde spirit, i.e., serenity (sérénité) is the overarching mood. After dinner, the married Vandevelde children, twins Tyl and Tylla, came with their spouses. I found it interesting that everyone, including the Vandeveldes, agreed that Paris had become dull, while Berlin was now the place to have fun. I hear this sentiment from all sides now.[16]

[14] Hugo Häring, 'Wie denkt und arbeitet der architektonische Nachwuchs?', *Baukunst und Werkform*, 5/5 (1952), pp. 15–22. In addition to his significant contributions to New Objectivity architecture, Hugo Häring is now recognised as a pioneer of 'organic' building, a movement that began in the 1920s and can be directly linked to Henry van de Velde's achievements starting in the mid-1890s.

[15] Cf. Nic Schubert, *Uttwil, das Dorf der Dichter und Maler* (Uttwil: Edition Frohsinn, 1985); in a 24 February 1988 letter to Wolf D. Pecher, Schubert, at an advanced age, recounted the commissions he had worked on up to 1931, including the built-in furniture for La Nouvelle Maison (Pecher estate, private collection).

[16] Harry Graf Kessler, *Tagebuch*, ed. Sabine Gruber und Ulrich Ott (Stuttgart: Cotta, 2010), vol. 9, entry Brussels, 19 May 1930, p. 352. Kessler had travelled by car from Paris to Brussels with his sister Wilma Marquise de Brion (1877–1963) and her eldest son, Jacques Marquis de Brion (1904–88). He drove back to Paris alone the next day. Wilma and Jacques then accompanied the artist to Kortrijk to inspect the new furniture that Henry van de Velde had designed for Wilma's Paris flat at 55 Avenue Kléber, which was produced by van de Velde's new Belgian partner, the furniture manufacturing company De Coene Frères.

When Henry van de Velde retired in 1936, it became urgent for the now 73-year-old to minimise the high costs associated with his daughter Nele's prolonged stays in the Binswanger clinic in Kreuzlingen. Having repeatedly questioned, and at times vehemently doubted, the necessity of ongoing treatment for over a decade, he ultimately acted against the doctors' strict advice and brought his eldest daughter, now 39, back into the care of her family.

As the Second World War broke out and the German Wehrmacht occupied Belgium, the house became quieter, particularly as Maria van de Velde became bedridden after suffering a stroke in October 1940 and was also seriously ill with diabetes. She passed away from a brain tumour on 27 July 1943.

To better understand the atmosphere at La Nouvelle Maison, let us turn once more to diarist Thea Sternheim, who visited father and daughter for the last time on 7 April 1944, following an initial visit on 27 March 1944 after a lengthy interruption:

Around noontime I take the tram to Tervueren to have lunch with Van de Veldes. It is almost comforting to spend the heavy hours away from the hustle and bustle of the city with a person who has been ground so thoroughly shaped by tragic fate as Nele. (...)
Lunch with Henri van de Velde and Nele. It is unfathomable that this lively, spirited man is now 82 years old [sic: 81]. The naturalness with which the meal unfolds (...) reminds me of the years we spent together on Lake Constance. (...)
Our sense of comfort seems to be mutual. Van de Velde says quite seriously: 'Stoisy, why don't you move in with us? For good? At my age of 82, death is just around the corner. What will happen to Nele then?' He puts his hand on my arm. 'Look after Nele when I'm gone. The child is very fond of you.' Suddenly, the affection I felt for the highly sensitive girl 25 or 20 years ago stands before us as a vivid reality. This is how I think our actions must appear to us at the last judgement (...).
We talk about the disaster that is Germany.
Van de Velde believes that Heinrich Mann's Der Untertan and the work of Sternheim resonate like prophecies today. (...)
The azalea at the window is unearthly, ecstatically white. (...)
As I say farewell, I think, 'This is probably the last time I see Van de Velde in this life', hugging him tightly.
In that moment, I recall my last visit to Aunt Lina in Cologne, when I too knew it was goodbye forever.
He embraces me again.
'This is for Maria van Rysselberghe,' he says.[17]

As a late act of 'revenge' by his still numerous opponents, Henry van de Velde was denounced as a German collaborator after the end of the war. The case was dismissed on 20 October 1945 as 'completely irrelevant' and he was rehabilitated. However, he was not formally informed of this by the Ministère de l'Instruction publique until over a year later, on 6 December 1946.[18] By that time, he had already decided to leave his latently hostile home country for good, despite Queen Dowager Elisabeth's attempts to change his mind during two visits. In the following months, he explored various options, and by winter 1946, the possibility of seeking final asylum in Switzerland reopened – just as it had in 1917 – thanks to his Swiss friend and patron Maja Sacher (1896–1989). In December 1945, he auctioned off the most valuable parts of his extensive library, which included numerous fine press editions and many books in luxury bindings. He donated another large collection of specialised literature to La Cambre, the school he had founded, keeping only a few essential books for writing his memoirs. In mid-July 1946, van de Velde sorted through his estate at home and, as he recounted in one of the many manuscripts of his autobiography, burned a wealth of files, manuscripts, plans, sketches, and models in the process.[19]

His move to Oberägeri, south of Zurich, with his daughter Nele on 9 September 1947 marked the beginning of the last chapter of Henry van de Velde's long and fulfilling life, which would last another ten years. He continued working on his final 'magnum opus', the *Récit de ma vie*, or 'Story of My Life,' which he had begun as early as 1917–1918 during his first exile in Switzerland – a congenial marvel of sparkling vitality, like so many of his artistic works.

[17] Sternheim, *Tagebücher 1903–1971* (see n. 8), entry Brussels, 7 April 1944, vol. 3, pp. 350–352. On 6 January 1947, she additionally refers to a meeting in Paris and recapitulates a recent visit by Maria van Rysselberghe (1866–1959) and André Gide (1869–1951) with van de Velde: *Early in the afternoon to Mme Rysselberghe. (...) She tells me about the trip to Brussels with Gide. About her visit with Henri van de Velde in Tervueren. She noted that the old friend had still seemed as friendly as ever but somehow worn. She had the impression that he was leading a melancholy life with Nele and that they were not doing well financially either. The house seemed slightly neglected.* Ibid., vol. 3, p. 503–4.

[18] According to a handwritten note by Hans Curjel in his estate at the DLA.

[19] As suggested by Marcel Gérard (1908 – after 1995), van de Velde's former assistant in Ghent, there was yet another occasion when records were destroyed. Cf. Ploegaerts 1999 (see n. 11), vol. 1, p. 526, and vol. 2, p. 705. Given the parts of his enormous estate that are preserved to this day in the Bibliothèque royale de Belgique, AML, and at the La Cambre school he founded in Brussels, it is difficult to estimate how extensive this collection must have once been, especially as van de Velde and his wife had also destroyed large quantities of documents or sold them as waste paper when they left Weimar in 1918–19.

Ground floor

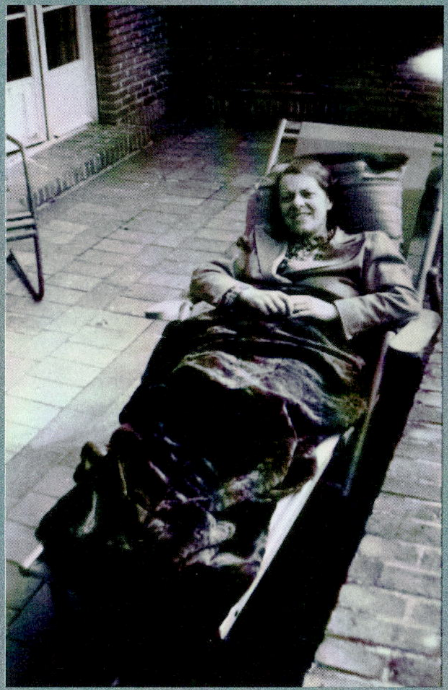

Henry van de Velde with family and friends

"The Making" and "The Maker"

Guido Stegen

Henry van de Velde's creations evolved to become increasingly resistant to interpretation through contemporary trends. La Nouvelle Maison is certainly a prime example of this. Its design is, to a degree, aligned with modernism due to its straightforwardness and the period in which it was conceived, yet it lacks the typical stylistic features associated with that movement. Van de Velde's unwavering commitment to functional and rational design consistently results in creations that appear organic, where the individual parts are subordinate to the whole. This holistic approach resonates with architect Louis Kahn's idea of 'listening carefully to what things want to be'. When elements are allowed to express their true nature, they exude essence, aesthetics, and poetry. Each design emerges from a unique interplay of context, needs, and requirements, making it surprisingly distinctive when permitted to be itself. As van de Velde famously stated, 'Rational design is both new and old. It leads to extremes, not a middle way.'

For van de Velde, rational design is merely the beginning of a long journey towards beauty. It represents the initial stage that, in his view, does not yield anything inherently beautiful or ugly; at this point, it remains neutral and must not exhibit difference, self-consciousness, pride, bias, stereotypes, or stereotypical styles. It exists without the desire to please. Only after reaching a stage of perfection does van de Velde confront the real challenge: making the rigidity of materials seem to vanish while reconciling functionality with materiality. Consequently, the knowledge and selection of materials are crucial. This approach means that, unlike other designs that promote rational and functional aesthetics, van de Velde's work consistently retains a surprisingly organic quality. The whole exudes a 'pose' that reveals the underlying forces and connections. Viewed from the entrance, La Nouvelle Maison's pose is sphinx-like .

Van de Velde developed his ideas about *la ligne*, the flowing line, to elucidate what occurs when matter and function are reconciled, and forcedness dissipates. This does not imply that the line must be either straight or crooked; rather, the line itself determines the form it wishes to take. Throughout his life, van de Velde aimed to refine the concept of 'the line':[1] only when the line is true does something achieve beauty. A similar principle can be found in Eastern philosophy, particularly in its application to art and printmaking, known as *wu wei*.[2] This concept describes an approach of 'not wanting', 'not doing', and 'not forcing'. Its practice is termed *wei wu wei*, or 'do not doing'. This challenging discipline requires the diligent abandonment of all forcedness and a detachment from the outcome. In design, it advocates for allowing the most suitable form to emerge – free from preconceived notions – one that perfectly fulfils its intended purpose while being stripped of all that is unnecessary and superfluous.

In van de Velde's work, the 'form that flows' is inextricably linked to continuity: the seamless transition of spaces, each flowing into the next, accompanied by a meticulous scenography that adds and reveals new areas at the right moment. Architecture provides connections in doses; it is suggestive and creates expectations, presenting within a larger whole the meaningful fragments that enable an understanding of what is yet to be revealed. This is known as intelligibility. It offers a mental comfort and a sense of security, referred to as 'situated understanding'. The careful orchestration of well-timed continuity, expectations, and suggestions is a truly distinctive quality of van de Velde's architectural oeuvre. It prompted Pierre Puttemans to remark that his architecture 'immediately makes you feel at home.'[3] In van de Velde's work, this existential need is also an integral part of the rational and functional design ethos: the need for a reassuring, safe, and predictable environment.

When I first became acquainted with La Nouvelle Maison decades ago, I encountered a common misconception about architecture: the tendency to describe it as merely an organisational chart of functions. Accounts of La Nouvelle Maison often state that, coming from the small hall, one enters the library, followed by the sitting area, and then reaches the dining room on the left and the studio on the right. While this is technically true based on the uses indicated on the plan, my initial experience revealed something different. This highlights an essential quality of Henry van de Velde's architecture. In his work, functionality serves the purpose of experience rather than abstract concepts like an organisational chart. The library does not create a barrier between me and the sitting area or the studio; together, they form a unified spatial experience, enriched by local sub-experiences, suggestions, and accents that spark curiosity and invite further

[1] Henry van de Velde, *Récit de ma vie 1917–57*, ed. Anne van Loo, with the assistance of Fabrice van de Kerckhove (Brussels/Turnhout: Versa-Brepols) 2023, vol. 3.2, pp.. 633–55.

[2] Henry van de Velde's early interest, shared with other artists and intellectuals of his time, in Eastern art and philosophy is well documented. This influence shaped his choices from the outset, serving as a foundation for his aesthetic principles. During this period, the concept of *wu wei* gained significant recognition in the West, both socially and politically. Lao Tzu's notion of non-action was explored in an 1893 essay by Tolstoy, which was later translated into French as 'Le non-agir'. Tolstoy was a prominent figure in cultural circles; between 1900 and 1909, he received eight nominations for the Nobel Prize in Literature and Peace. This was also the formative period of the Kunstgewerbeschule in Weimar, led by van de Velde, who advocated for a responsive, rational, and functional approach to design, rooted in essential needs and material characteristics. For van de Velde, this attitude of adaptation and acceptance held significant socio-political implications, reflecting his beliefs in pacifism and anarchism.

[3] Pierre Puttemans and Léon Ploegaerts, *L'œuvre architecturale de Henry van de Velde* (Brussels and Quebec: Vokaer and Presse de l'Université de Laval, 1987).

Compared to other rational and functional designs, van de Velde's work is always strikingly organic. Overall, it has a 'pose' that, on the entrance side of La Nouvelle Maison, is almost sphinx-like.

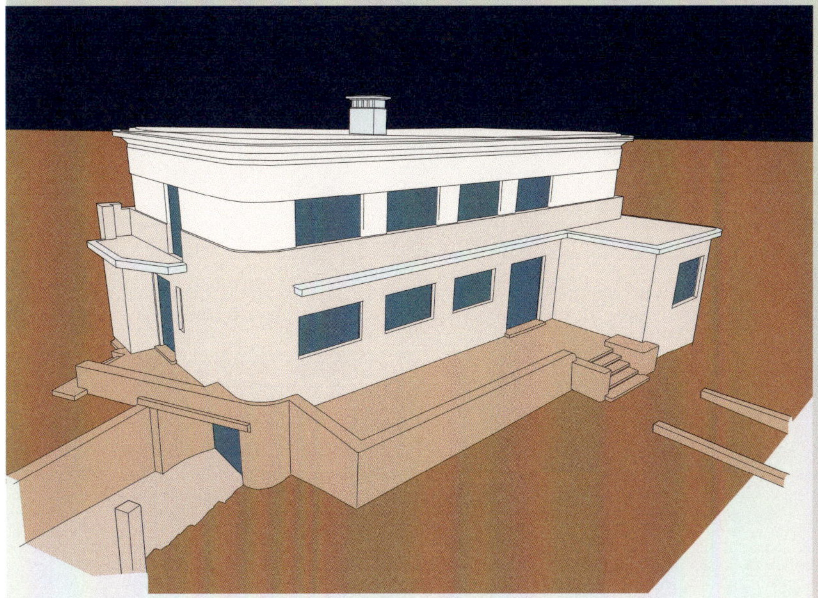

Drawing of Henry van de Velde by Théo van Rysselberghe.

exploration. The journey continues and gradually reveals an increasingly complete narrative of the house. Yet, despite the changing nature of the immediate environment, one experience remains constant: the endpoint of the long axis that stretches from the hall to the furthest exterior wall of the studio. This point is the most significant constant in both time and space. Metrically, it represents the longest possible distance visible indoors between two exterior walls. At the terminus of this axis, in the studio, hangs the portrait painted by Théo van Rysselberghe in 1891 of Maria Sèthe, who would later become van de Velde's wife. Architecture is not merely an organisational chart; the library and sitting area do not isolate me from the painting. Instead, they extend the time during which I remain directly connected to this artwork.

This is just one case example of the constants in van de Velde's architectural work: his designs are compositions of relationships and experiences. This leads to ground plans that may appear unusual until one engages directly with the buildings. In La Nouvelle Maison, the components are surprisingly unpretentious. Everything is attuned to the organic whole. A heritage building of such exceptional quality suffers quickly in restoration when one does not step back far enough to maintain a clear perspective on the bigger picture. In the initial phase, when all authenticity is still murky, there is only a vague notion of the intended direction. This notion must be continually refined. Restorers do not hold preconceived opinions about aesthetics; their focus is on balance. They do not force changes but rather follow the natural progression of the restoration process.

In his memoirs, Henry van de Velde wrote little about La Nouvelle Maison; it was the most modest and smallest private residence he designed for his family.[4] Whether by coincidence or not, the austere, streamlined, and rational design aligns perfectly with the precarious financial situation the van de Velde-Sèthe family faced upon their return to Belgium and during the house's construction.

A design attitude of 'adapting' necessitates the absence of a prior 'visionary' core concept. Core concepts emerge from careful listening to needs and constraints, observing how they influence form; they may compete with one another or overlap. The challenge lies in reconciling these contradictions to create a perfect whole – a 'wholeness' – and, for its sake, making only strictly necessary concessions in the conception of the parts: this is the art of imperfection.

Balance and wholeness defy description; they represent a simultaneous experience of relationships and connections across multiple dimensions and through all the senses. Attempting to describe this can isolate a core concept from the whole, which is detrimental. Nevertheless, allow me to illustrate several core concepts based on a single statement van de Velde made about La Nouvelle Maison in a 1940 publication:

> **It is an architecture reduced to masses,**
> **a dialogue of solids and voids; an architecture**
> **deeply rooted in the ground,**
> **as if it were the very fruit of it … .[5]**

It is relatively unimportant to determine whether these ideas originated during the design process or were a later realisation of what the design ultimately became. This statement already points to some essential aspects of La Nouvelle Maison's architecture.

… reduced to masses …

The architectural expression of gravity acting on the mass of a structure is known as tectonics. This manifestation of the universal force to which we are all subject reflects our own experiences.[6] It encompasses stacking and tension, how the structure resists forces, and the flow of these forces, as well as stability and rest. It manifests itself in a vertical continuity of matter. There is no shortage of mass here; the shape of the house appears as if it were kneaded from clay. The detailing is austere and executed in the same brick, resulting in a very solid appearance. Both externally and internally, it is an exercise in subtractive design.[7]

The volumetric effect of the house begins with a basic volume of 17 metres by 8.2 metres, with rounded corners that are fully visible on the first storey. This defines the house against the sky, presenting a simple and massive silhouette. As you move downward, the mass becomes more organic, shaped in response to the horizontal functional connections with its surroundings. At garden level, garden walls – crafted from the same clay-coloured

[4] Van de Velde designed four houses for the van de Velde-Sèthe family: Bloemenwerf, 1895, in Uccle; Hohe Papeln, 1906, in Weimar; de Tent, 1920, in Wassenaar; La Nouvelle Maison, 1928, in Tervuren.

[5] Henry van de Velde, 'L'architecture d'aujourd'hui en regard de celle du passé', Reconstruction, vol. 1, no. 4 (December 1940), pp. 15–22.

[6] In *Pages de doctrines* from 1942, van de Velde reflects with some uncertainty on the connection between the observer, the designer, and the objects that experience the same forces. He states, 'Illusion, I know, but it is undeniable that I truly feel […] the drama of materials subjected to the play of forces.' Henry van de Velde, *Pages de doctrines* (Dilbeek: Cahiers d'architecture et d'urbanisme), pp. 95–97.

[7] Subtractive design involves starting with a single material or block, whether hard or malleable, from which volumes are removed through chiselling, cutting, and filing. This contrasts with additive design, which focuses on accumulation and addition. In subtractive architecture, the concave quality of the space predominates, while in additive architecture, the convex quality takes centre stage.
For instance, Rietveld's Schröder House exemplifies additive design, whereas La Nouvelle Maison leans towards subtractive principles. It 'leans towards' because Henry van de Velde also treats the single mass as malleable in the delicate extensions that connect to the garden. Throughout his work, he has demonstrated a strong affinity for subtractive, moulding design, a hallmark of which is the systematic use of rounded corners, both on external and internal edges. This effect is further accentuated by the uniformity of colour between ceilings and walls.

At the endpoint of the long axis between the hall and studio hangs the portrait of Maria Sèthe (painted by Théo van Rysselberghe in 1891).

Van de Velde's spaces are 'embracing' and place the human being at the centre. This embroidered tapestry, produced during his years of artistic crisis before his turn to architectural design with the Villa Bloemenwerf in 1895, already revealed a non-Euclidean perception of space. Space, due to our presence and perception, pushes matter aside; straight lines curve; and, as we move, matter recedes.

The shape of the house appears as if it were kneaded from clay. The detailing is austere and executed in the same brick.

material – facilitate outdoor use. The horizontal solid registers of the house, which become 'thicker' as they approach the ground, emphasise its heaviness and tectonic qualities. Even in the least articulated northeast façade, these horizontal registers remain subtly visible.

There is one spot that has captured the attention of photographers since the early days of La Nouvelle Maison, where the tectonic expression is most striking: the western corner on the street side.[8] Here, the rounded corner of the basic volume remains visible as it seamlessly merges into the ground, while the design reveals a cross-section of the organically added layers, because the tectonic there is most powerful: the western corner on the street side.

... dialogue of solids and voids ...

This concerns horizontal spatial continuity. Nothing illustrates this better than van de Velde himself, who recounts in his memoirs his first foray into architecture. Regarding the design of Bloemenwerf in Uccle in 1895, he states, 'I had no trouble placing the openings in the right place'.[9] The placement of openings is tied to the careful listening to where and how the spatial relationships wish to manifest. Van de Velde accomplishes this flawlessly because, rather than focusing solely on the plan, he maintains a vision of the continuity of space. The 'dialogue of solids and voids' fluidly narrates the house, enriching the relationships and views with varying degrees of openness and intimacy, tailored to the protective needs inherent in each use and activity.

Light and artworks play a crucial role in the scenography of spatial continuity. Daylight enables the flow of space, and at the end of a vista, one encounters both light and a view. The few exceptions where vistas terminate at blank walls are designed to highlight a piece of art. The relationships on the ground floor create an elongated loop, with two parallel main axes supporting different uses and providing views of the two distinct gardens.

... deeply rooted in the ground, as if it were the very fruit of it ...

Here, van de Velde addresses form, colour, and texture. The colour and texture of the sand-coated brick reference the local clay, while the smooth transition between the ground and the architecture is realised in the solid concave plinth.

The choice of brick was of such importance to Henry van de Velde that, when he finally found the perfect façade brick,[10] he adapted the design to fit its module.[11] The hue of the brick varies in NCS coding between -Y20R and -Y40R,[12] with the colour vividness and saturation closely aligning with 4010 in NCS coding.[13] This decision influenced all the horizontal dimensions of the façades, as well as some of the interior walls.[14]

There are two types of facing bricks, façade bricks and clinker bricks, both featuring the same sand-coating and sourced from the same brickworks.[15] Each serves a different technical role and has distinct dimensions. The clinker brick measures 210 × 95 × 50 mm and is fired at a higher temperature; it is used for areas most exposed to rain, moisture, and frost, such as the structures at the transition from the façades to the garden. The façade brick measures 215 × 105 × 40 mm and is fired at a lower temperature. It is employed for the outer skin of the heated volume of the house and has proven effective even in today's climate change-related heavy, driving rains due to its excellent water buffering capacity and rapid evaporation.[16]

In principle, these two brick formats allow for the use of the same brick modulation of 60 mm in height, but in the case of La Nouvelle Maison, this was consistently not implemented. The preliminary investigations and the planning evolution study provide no clear explanation for this choice, other than perhaps a preference for a wider joint (of 25 mm) that creates a shadow line in the joints, similar to that of the façade brick.

For La Nouvelle Maison, the colour of the brick that connects with the ground serves as the foundational shade for the entire colour palette. This creates the impression that the whole house is modelled from a single substance, one material. The consistent base tone instils a sense of calm and stability.[17] For van de Velde, the line or shape is always the primary means of imparting lightness to the mass, a process he refers to as 'dematerialisation.' Colour supports this aim and functions to express spatial continuity.[18]

The walls, ceilings, carpeting, and the colour choices for the fixed furniture in La Nouvelle Maison exhibit varying nuances of the brick shade. The interior colours are paler, and as they fade, they become less saturated.[19] Alongside this foundational hue and the changing shades, van de Velde introduces a third dimension

[8] The basic volume is tilted at an angle of 30 degrees in relation to Albertlaan, unlike in the initial sketches. This adjustment positions the corner closest to the street, giving it a monumental presence. The tilt enhances the visibility of the façades in foreshortening, enabling one to appreciate the full mass of the basic volume.

[9] See also G. Stegen, 'Bloemenwerf en het portret van Maria Sèthe', Brussel Erfgoed, 29 (December 2018). This article goes into greater depth regarding the design process and 'placing the openings in the right position'.

[10] The Belvedere façade brick is a sand-coated hand-moulded brick with a yellowish core and grey-pink sand finish from the region north of Maastricht.

[11] The notes regarding the changes for the façade brick are kept in the Fonds van de Velde, La Cambre. The calculations for these new dimensions are found in handwritten documents (005.R16526Nd427_13 and 006.R_16526Nd428_13). The comparison of the old and new dimensions, for the purpose of studying the impact on the project, is noted in documents with annotations in red (024.R_16526Nd457_14 and 025.R_16526Nd458_14). These documents are undated. Relative dating indicates that they were created between 20 April and 18 May 1928.

[12] NCS = Natural Colour System. The format of an NCS code is ####-####. The first group of four characters denotes the shade; the second group denotes the hue in the colour wheel. For example, a colour between -Y20R and -Y40R indicates a yellowish (Y) hue containing 20 to 40% red (R).

[13] Shade 4010 indicates 40% light absorption and 10% colour saturation. This figure is an average, as the sand coating, which consists of a mixture of white-grey and pink sand, makes the shade highly dependent on light and humidity. These conditions significantly influence the transparency and reflection of the sand grains. The shade is 4010, measured in clear overcast weather; variations range from 3010 (dry and sunny) to 6010 (humid).

[14] The horizontal dimensions changed to a module of 11 cm. The vertical dimensions remained unchanged, as the previous façade brick also had a course height of 60 mm (40 mm brick and 20 mm joint). The height dimensions are indicated on the plans with detailed information on the number of courses (T, from French 'tas'). For example, for the intervening masonry, ending with a supplementary end joint of 2cm: 69T × 6 = 414 + 2 = 416 cm.

[15] The sand coating is crucial, as it adjusts the yellowish core to the appropriate pinkish hue. The core of the façade brick varies in colour from 3020-Y10R to 3020-Y20R, while the core of the clinker brick ranges from 4030-Y to 5020-G80Y, leaning towards an olive-green tone due to the high firing temperature. Nevertheless, when treated with the specific sand coating, both types of brick achieve a nearly identical shade when dry. The subtle shift towards a redder tone imparts a sense of calm, added mass, and greater weight to the façade, grounding it more firmly to the clay and enhancing its harmony with the dark green of the exterior joinery.

[16] Thanks to the façade's effective water management and buffering capacity, the masonry remained functionally undamaged even after more than ninety years. Research revealed that the original laying and joint mortars were specifically adapted to the nature and requirements of each type of brick: a softer mortar for the façade brick and a harder, water-resistant mortar for the brick. The damage observed in the clinker brick masonry was largely due to the use of inappropriate mortar during past repairs, which led to a rapid escalation of damage from water infiltrations within the wall cores.

[17] Henry van de Velde does not consistently use colour properties – hue, brightness, saturation, and gloss – to prioritise continuity. For instance, in Bloemenwerf, his first house, it is the uniformity in shade (brightness and saturation) across the rich hue palette that creates a sense of calm and continuity, while the colours themselves help to dematerialise the mass. See G. Stegen, 'Licht, kleur en vorm in Bloemenwerf en La Nouvelle Maison', paper presented at the BRK-APROA Colloquium titled Nieuwe kijk op oude kleur in de conservatie-restauratie, 16–17 November 2023.

[18] Ibid.

[19] This is a general principle: to maintain the impression of constant colour saturation, saturation must decrease as brightness increases. This phenomenon relates to the colour sensitivity of the eye's cones in relation to the brightness perceived by the rods.

Starting from the simple base volume with rounded corners, the mass becomes more organic, starting to form horizontal connections with its surroundings.

The western corner on the street side that captured the attention of photographers.

The colour and texture of the sand-coated brick make reference to the local clay.

In all his work, van de Velde demonstrated a strong affinity for a substractive, moulding design. A hallmark of this is his systematic use of rounded corners, as seen in the plinth of La Nouvelle Maison, which makes it appear 'as if it were the very fruit of it'.

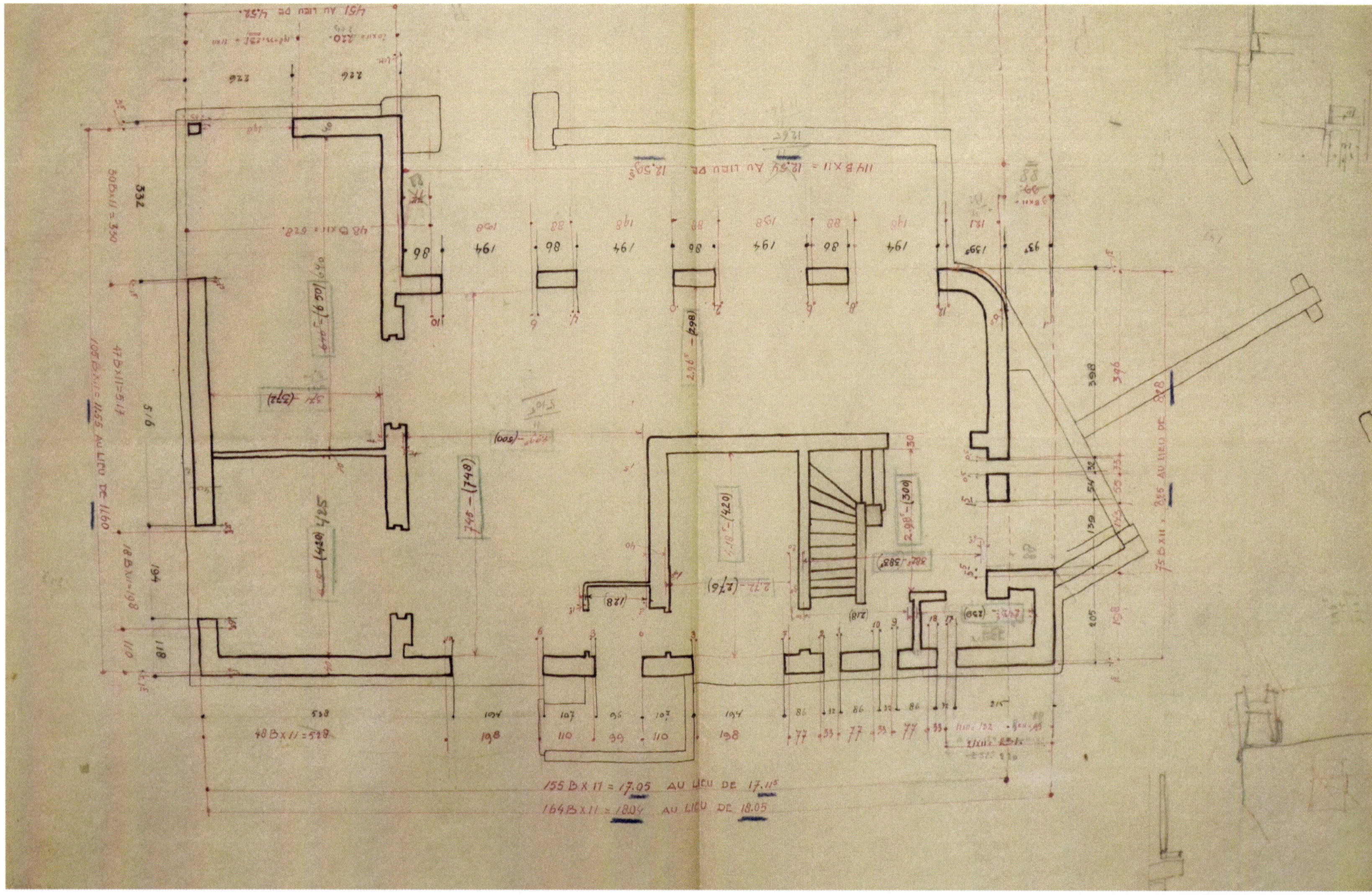

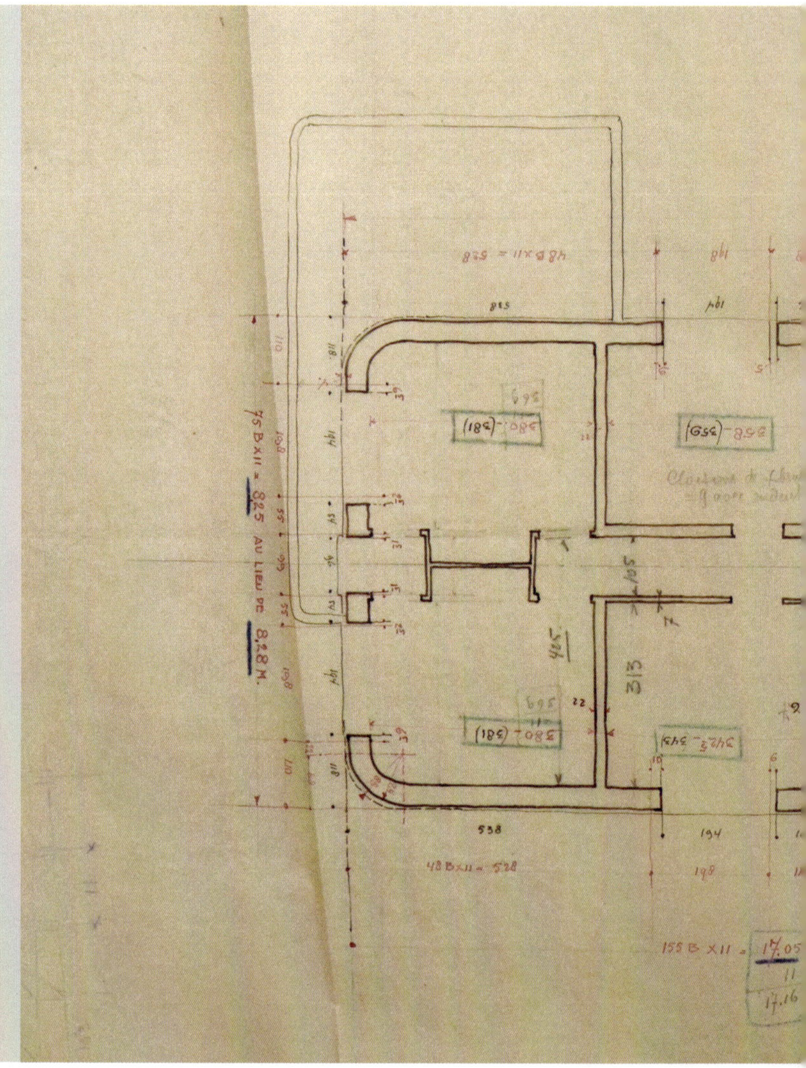

The vertical modulation remained unchanged. The drawing already includes the dual modulation for the façade brick (6 cm) and the clinker brick (7.5 cm).

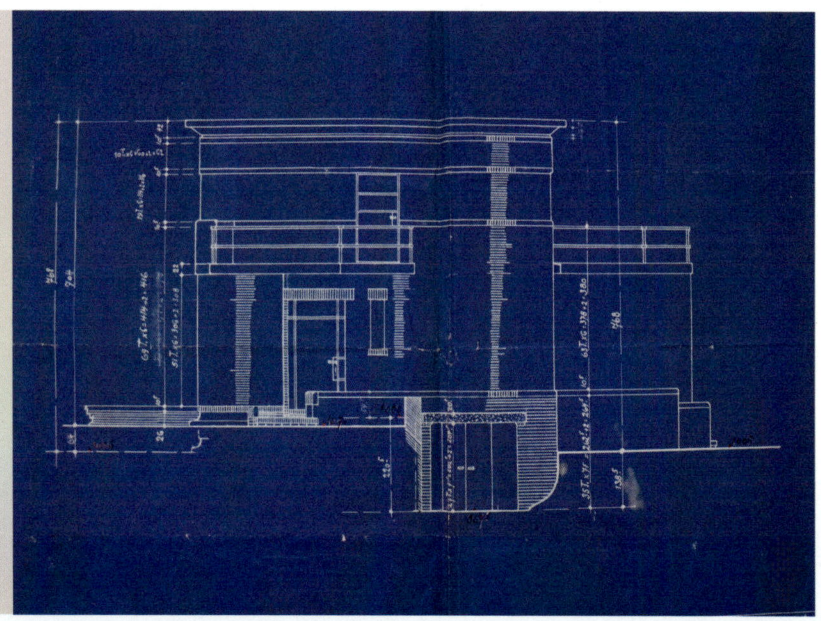

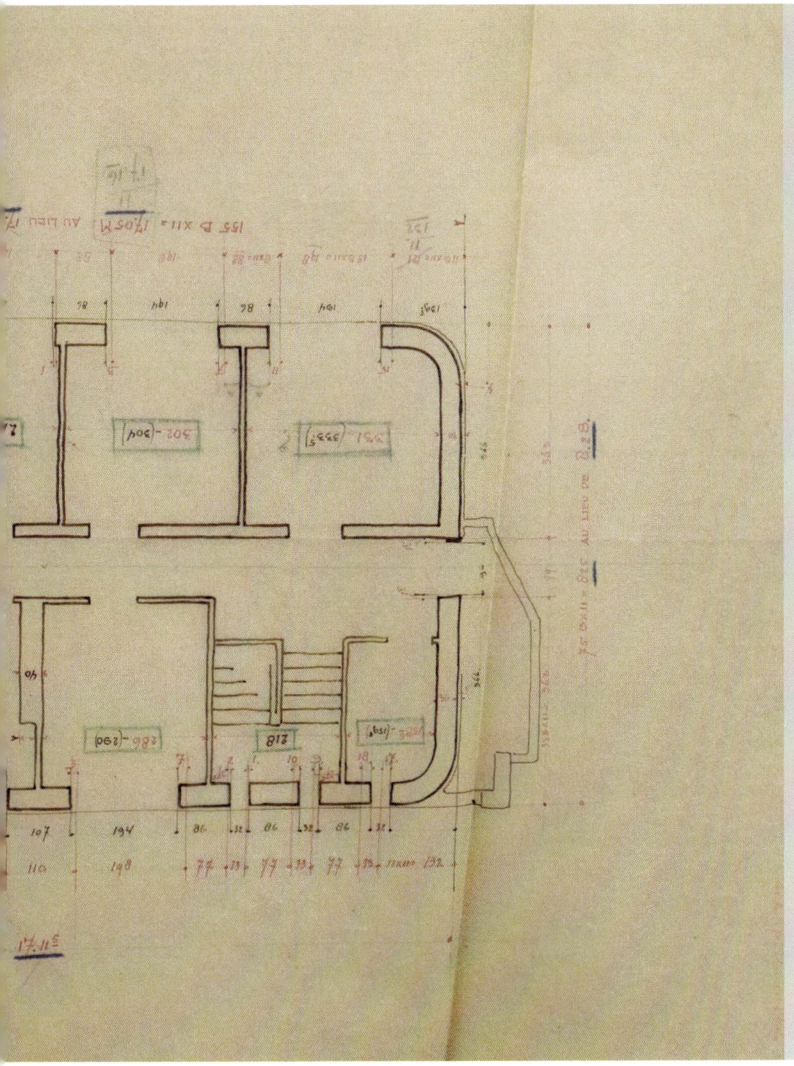

The plans from the original building dossier in the Fonds van de Velde at La Cambre include a handwritten comparison of the old dimensions and the new ones which arose from the change in façade brick.

The façade modulation resulting from the choice of the new Belvedere façade brick. In the centre, the façade brick. On the left, the clinker brick as it is intended to be used, aligning with the modules of the façade brick. On the right, the clinker brick as used in La Nouvelle Maison, featuring a wide shadow joint.

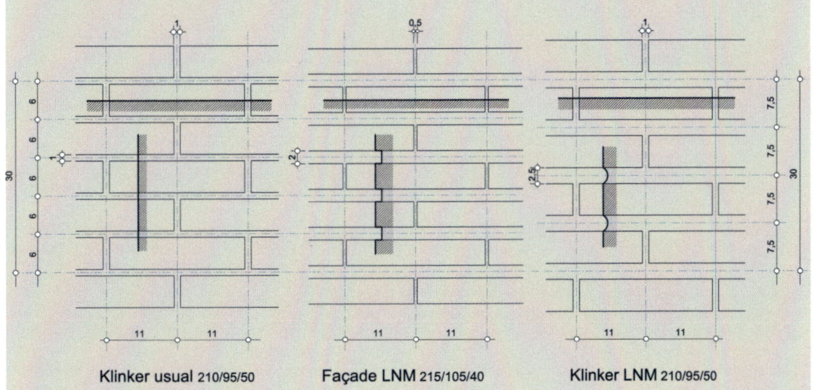

The use of clinker bricks with wide joints occasionally leads to deviations in the modulation and connection issues between the façade and clinker brickwork, as seen here at the junction of the terrace and the façade.

The palette of colours and materials. Top centre: façade materials and colours. Bottom: interior paint colours (walls, windows, doors, and exterior surfaces of joinery, etc.). Top left: flooring. Top right: interior surfaces of built-in furnishings.

The gloss levels range from 5% to 40%.

to dematerialise mass: the gloss value.[20] Surface finishes range from semi-gloss to completely matte, even within the same colour and shade. The gloss value is an independent variable, resulting in a mass that loses its solid appearance and takes on a playful, dynamic quality. Van de Velde refers to this method of creating a dynamic surface as 'dynamographique'.[21]

-Y30R is known to be a particularly unstable colour, a perfectly flexible shade of ochre that can take on various forms depending on the light and surrounding colours. An error in mixing the colour can diminish its dynamic effect.[22] Experiencing the house reveals the full extent of La Nouvelle Maison's highly dynamic character; one never tires of it. The house absorbs and softens the changing seasons, the weather, and the daily cycles. Within its walls, one never feels confined. The house offers new surprises each day.

In this universe of continuity, where dynamic spaces flow from the outside in, bathed in the soft nuances of the ubiquitous -Y20R to -Y40R hues, La Nouvelle Maison surprises with bursts of bright, saturated colours that mark endpoints, the house's most interior and intimate spots. This intensity is vividly present in the warm yellow of the kitchen, the interiors of the fixed furniture, and in artworks positioned at key endpoints, or stopping points, within the spatial system. Intense colour manifests in depth, both metrically and topologically.[23]

Art and Architecture

The van de Velde-Sèthe family had to cover a third of the construction costs of La Nouvelle Maison by selling artworks from their collection[24] – pieces that, aside from their artistic value, were poignant reminders of personal relationships, influences, and interests. In their homes, art objects were not merely interchangeable; they played a significant architectural role.[25] A functional arrangement of an object requires a relationship between being notable and being noticed.[26] Being notable is a characteristic of the installed object, while being noticed depends on the spatial configuration surrounding its placement. In the case of La Nouvelle Maison, there are several key areas where this close relationship exists – spaces that are essential to the overall spatial experience of the house. The way these areas function within the whole is related to the 'dialogue of solids and voids', as van de Velde describes it.

Three locations are static (S1, S2, and S3 in the image). The artworks in these spots hang on a 'solid' that marks the endpoint of a long axis of sight and movement, surrounded by much activity, making them highly noticeable. Their presence is significant, further emphasised by their greater vibrancy compared to the surroundings. Among the three art objects that define their locations from a 'solid', Maria Sèthe's portrait (S1) has the most substantial impact, owing to the extended space (the axis) from which the painting is observed.

[20] In La Nouvelle Maison, the gloss level varies from 5% to 40%, depending on the materials and types of paint, and is measured as an 'indicative' gloss level in accordance with ISO 2813-60°. The Moha limestone and terrazzo floors and steps have a gloss level of 25–30%. Distemper and lime paint finishes reach a maximum gloss of 5% once fully dried. Meanwhile, synthetic paints, oil-based finishes, and wax layers fall within the 15% to 30% range.

[21] An early quote from van de Velde about wall finishes using wallpaper offers some insight into his pursuit of dematerialisation and dynamism: 'to conceal the cold nakedness of the wall, its hostility and its threat to crush us ...'.

[22] A shift towards the yellow side can cause the colour to look dirty when influenced by surrounding greens. In contrast, a shift towards red makes the colour look muted and greyish when affected by greens.

[23] Metric distance is indicated in metres; topological distance is measured by the number of changes in direction or view.

[24] J. Vansteenkiste, 'Bouwhistorische studie voor de restauratie van La Nouvelle Maison', p. LNM_VS_002, p. 9.

[25] G. Stegen, 'Bloemenwerf en het portret van Maria Sèthe', in *Brussel Erfgoed* 29 (December 2018).

[26] When there is a strong correlation between how remarkable something is and how much it is noticed in complex spatial environments, such as cities, the environment feels readable and comprehensible, and therefore safe.

'The ultimate interior': the vibrant colours of the kitchen and the insides of the cupboards deviate from the concept of 'shades of the same hue'.

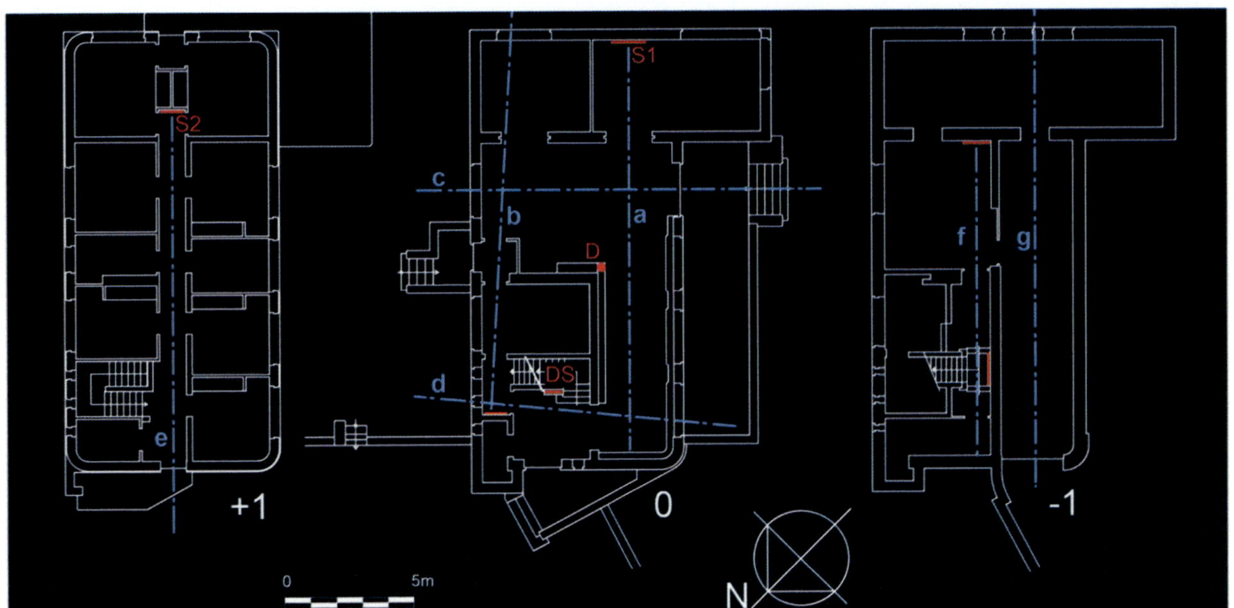

Architectural, monumental arrangements in relation to the house's long sightlines: axes 'a' through 'g' according to the original state (1928) of the house. These axes form the primary framework of the relationships within the house.

The Koninklijk Museum voor Schone Kunsten in Antwerp (KMSKA) acquired this painting from Henry van de Velde in 1949, and it is now part of the permanent exhibition in the renovated museum. Recognising the painting's architectural significance to La Nouvelle Maison, and the museum's commitment to presenting art in context, an agreement was reached between the museum and the owner of La Nouvelle Maison to create a 3D facsimile to take the place of the original painting within the house.[27]

One art object (D1) is entirely dynamic: an 1898 plaster study by George Minne (1866–1941), which the artist gifted to Henry van de Velde, anticipating that the project for a fountain featuring five similar figures would not come to fruition.[28] This renowned kneeling figure was later realised in various materials and poses, and, at van de Velde's instigation, the fountain was eventually created in marble for the Osthaus Museum (now Museum Folkwang) in Hagen. The sculpture was prominently displayed in van de Velde's other residences. In La Nouvelle Maison, it is centrally positioned; the library bookcase has been extended alongside the fireplace to ensure the sculpture is visible from a wide area. Its placement near the convex corner of the L-shaped living space further enhances its visibility as one moves about. The colour of the sculpture aligns with the architectural colour scheme: it matches the colour of the library bookcase and the walls, falling within the gentle shades of the façade brick colour. It plays a sculptural dynamic role, as the background shifts and changes in response to the observer's movement.

DS is both static and dynamic at the same time. It is a bas-relief made of nearly black stone by the young Willia Menzel (1907–95).[29] Created while La Nouvelle Maison was under construction, it remained in the house until after Henry van de Velde's death, attached to its pedestal by a metal bracket. Although the frontal axis in the hall is short, the relief is visible from outside through the glass of the front door. Its dark colour and semi-gloss finish enhance its three-dimensionality, allowing it to function effectively in the small entrance hall, which serves as a pass-through space with oblique views of the intricate relief.

The composition of the house was clearly designed with S1 and D1 in mind. Regarding the bas-relief DS, the initial plans for the house already indicated a pedestal in that location, likely intended for a freestanding object.[30] In the final detailed plans for the construction of the staircase, the pedestal is wide, shallow and higher, tailored specifically for the bas-relief.

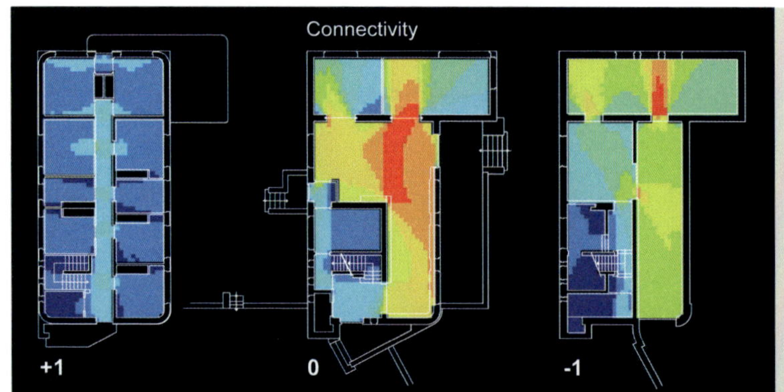

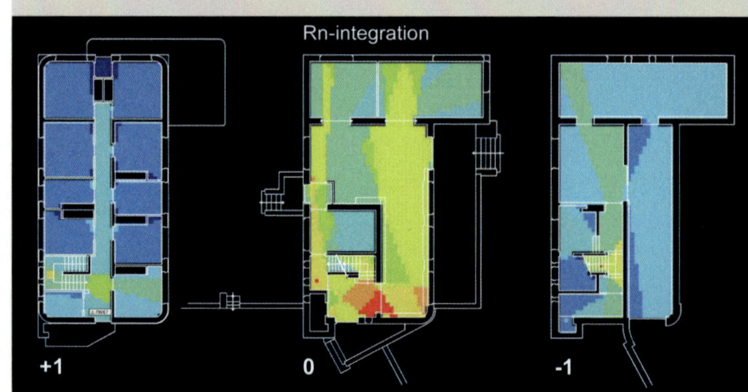

A spatial analysis using VGA (Visibility Graph Analysis, © Space Syntax). This software analyses form and allows for the visualisation of spatial properties and the prediction of how they will affect human behaviour and preferences within a given space. It also offers an objective means of confirming what we often intuitively perceive or suspect. These images help analytically understand the mental comfort one would feel in La Nouvelle Maison. The specific images shown here highlight areas of centrality. Warm colours (red, ochre) indicate higher centrality, while cool colours (blue, green) signify lower centrality.

VGA connectivity of the ground level. Connectivity is best understood as a form of static centrality. Red represents the area from which the most space is visible, providing the best overall view – in this case, the ground level. The red/orange zone is located at the intersection of the 'a' and 'c' axes. This spot not only offers the best overview of the interior space but also provides views of both gardens on either side of the house. It is assumed that quality arises when local and global significance align. Additionally, this zone offers a view of the artworks D (Minne) and S1 (van Rysselberghe), giving them a monumental prominence.

VGA-Rn of all cooperating building layers. Rn integration is best understood as a dynamic centrality: how central are the locations in relation to all spatial connections throughout the house. The red or ochre areas indicate the places where people move the most. Again, there is a local/global synergy: the internal centrality of the private spaces aligns with the connection to the public space. At the same time, axes a (the slow residential axis) and b (the fast "service" axis) emerge as dynamic zones.

[27] The facsimile was produced by Factum Arte in Madrid. Like the original, the copy is composed of three parts: the central canvas section, the wooden passe-partout partially painted in an impressionistic style, and the gilded wooden frame.

[28] The van de Velde-Sèthe family Minne's study while they were still living in the Bloemenwerf house in Uccle. It can be seen in many photographs from that period before 1900.

[29] According to François Hers, who was acquainted with the work in La Nouvelle Maison during the time the Hers family resided there, the bas-relief can be seen in published photographs of the entrance hall; it appears dark and semi-glossy.

[30] In the initial plans, the pedestal was square instead of wide and shallow.

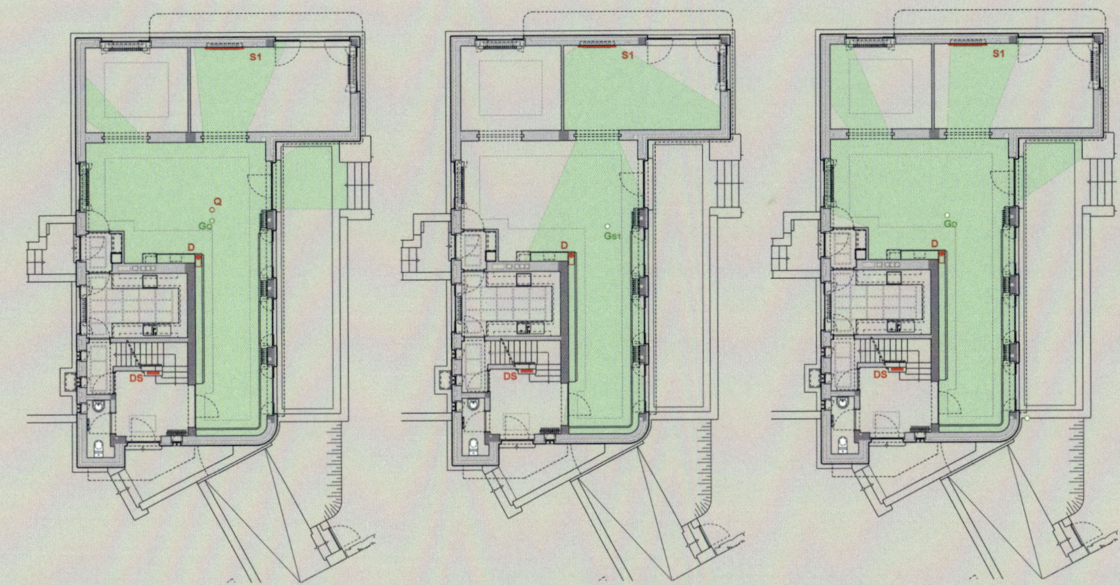

When we check the range of the visual field from a single point (viewpoint Q) in the red zone of connectivity, we find that not only is the visual field large, but also that the focal point of the visual field is close to the viewpoint, further underlining its static nature.

We can also view the space from the perspective of the artworks, in this case, the painting by van Rysselberghe. The 'a' axis then immediately comes into view. However, the focal point of this visibility field also lies within the zone of highest static centrality. The arrangement and architecture ensure that a natural distance is maintained from the painting.

Due to its central placement, and irrespective of the angle, Minne's sculpture has the largest visibility field. Here, too, the focal point of that field lies within the red zone of highest static centrality, but now near the artwork, which is also what a sculpture demands.

The endpoint of the long axis, coming from the entrance.

Central placement of Minne's work (D1).
Historical photo: date c. 1930,
author unknown.

The entrance hall where the bas-relief by Willia Menzel was placed on the pedestal.

The plaster study for the bas-relief DS.

The Garden

The original state of the garden is well-documented in historical photographs, which enable the identification of the plantings. While no garden construction plans are available, a schematic drawing from a publication provides some insight.[31] Additionally, a small implementation plan created during the design stage includes instructions in pencil for soil movements.[32]

The elongated triangular plot results from the merging of two original lots. Bordered by streets, it measures 97.50 m in length and 43.50 m in width, with a maximum level difference of 2.50 m. The house is positioned centrally within the triangle, straddling the boundary between the two lots. This oblong structure stands at a right angle to the plot, effectively dividing it into two gardens: one to the northeast and the other to the southwest. The entrance to the plot is located on the short northwest side of the house, providing direct access to both gardens. At the time of construction, Albertlaan (the entrance) was still a dirt road, while the other two cobbled streets were already established. Before the house was built, a ditch ran across the plot from the current entrance to the northeast corner, where functional access to the garden existed.[33] This ditch was partially enclosed with tubing and remains essential for the natural drainage of surface water, soil moisture, and the type of plantings. Given the changing climate, maintaining this drainage system is increasingly vital for the hassle-free conservation of La Nouvelle Maison.

The garden features three distinct usage zones, a requirement that the van de Velde-Sèthe family had in mind even before acquiring the plot. In his correspondence, Henry reached out to friends assisting with the search, specifying the need for land that could accommodate a meadow, an orchard, and a vegetable garden.

The highest point of the site is located at the northern corner, from which the ground gently slopes down towards the southeast, where the orchard was established. In the lowest and wettest area on the same side of the house lay the kitchen garden. The northern edge of the plot featured a tree line that acted as a buffer against the cold. The elongated, pointed southwestern section of the garden served as the meadow. During the garden's design, the natural topography was, wherever feasible, transformed into horizontal terraces, clearly defined by visible banks. Close to the façades, horizontal lawns extended up to the rounded concrete base of the house. The entire triangular garden was enclosed by a hedge, with the exception of the entrance.

La Nouvelle Maison's garden is organically connected to the house, embodying the concept of *la ligne* in full effect. There exists a strong visual and functional interaction, enhanced by low garden walls and terraces. The kitchen seamlessly communicates with the kitchen garden, orchard, and household functions.[34] The library and studio overlook the meadow, framed by the Avenue de Tervueren and, beyond it, the Sonian Forest and the Arboretum. The sitting area, featuring a piano and fireplace, serves as a pivotal point within the overall layout, providing a view of both gardens.

[31] Planting plan with garden diagram included in the schematic plans of La Nouvelle Maison, published in *La Cité*, 5–6 (April–May 1933), a special issue devoted to Henry van de Velde.

[32] Document number in the digitised archive of La Nouvelle Maison, La Cambre: 013.R_16526Nd439_8.

[33] Document number in the digitised archive of La Nouvelle Maison, La Cambre: 009.R_16526Nd434. The ditch or stream is marked 'fossé'.

[34] The bleaching meadow with wash line, the herb garden, the rainwater pump, etc., concealed from view by a hedge.

Excerpt from the new development of the district, with new building lines and mention of the culverted ditch (fossé). Added in red is the final placement of La Nouvelle Maison. Also noted across the new 'avenue' is 'R. Verwilghen', the plot and house of architect Raphaël Verwilghen, who oversaw the construction of La Nouvelle Maison for van de Velde, was a co-manager of the construction company, and was responsible for the concrete construction plans and execution drawings. He ran an architectural firm with architect J.-J. Eggericx, who at the time was engaged in the research and development of garden suburbs such as Le Logis & Floréal. From 1927, both were also lecturers at the La Cambre design school founded by Henry van de Velde.

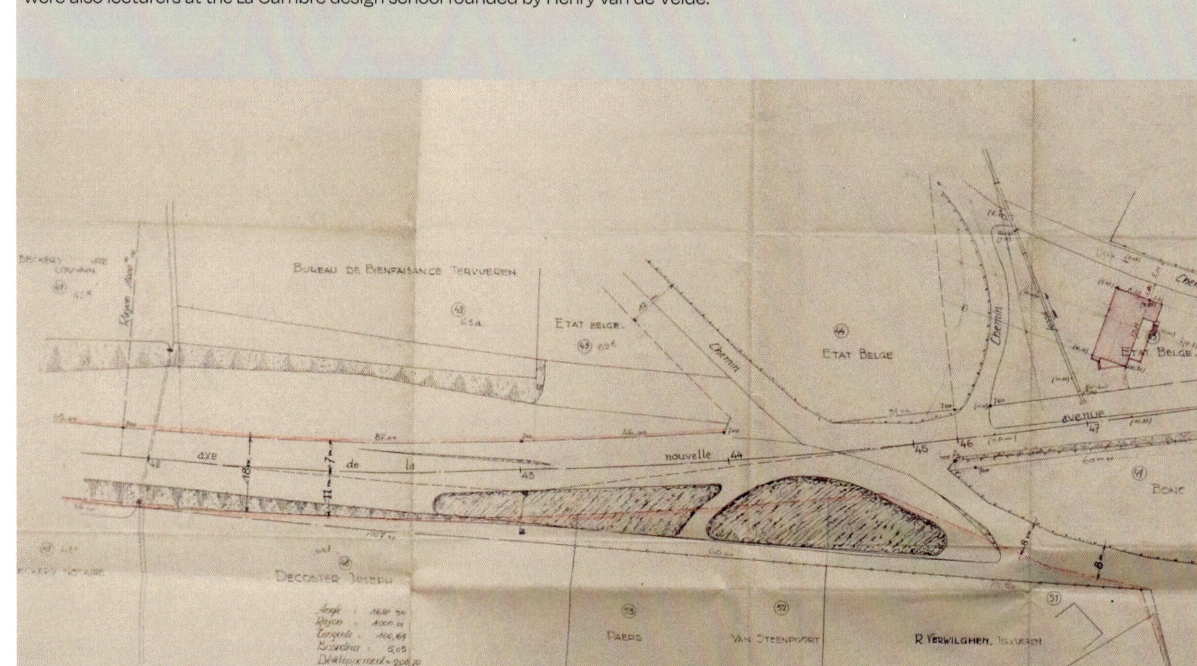

La Nouvelle Maison was built in the green, wooded eastern periphery of Brussels, now part of the Flemish Region. It was originally part of the Sonian Forest. Despite further subdivision and expansion around the centre of Tervuren, the house remains situated in mostly green surroundings.

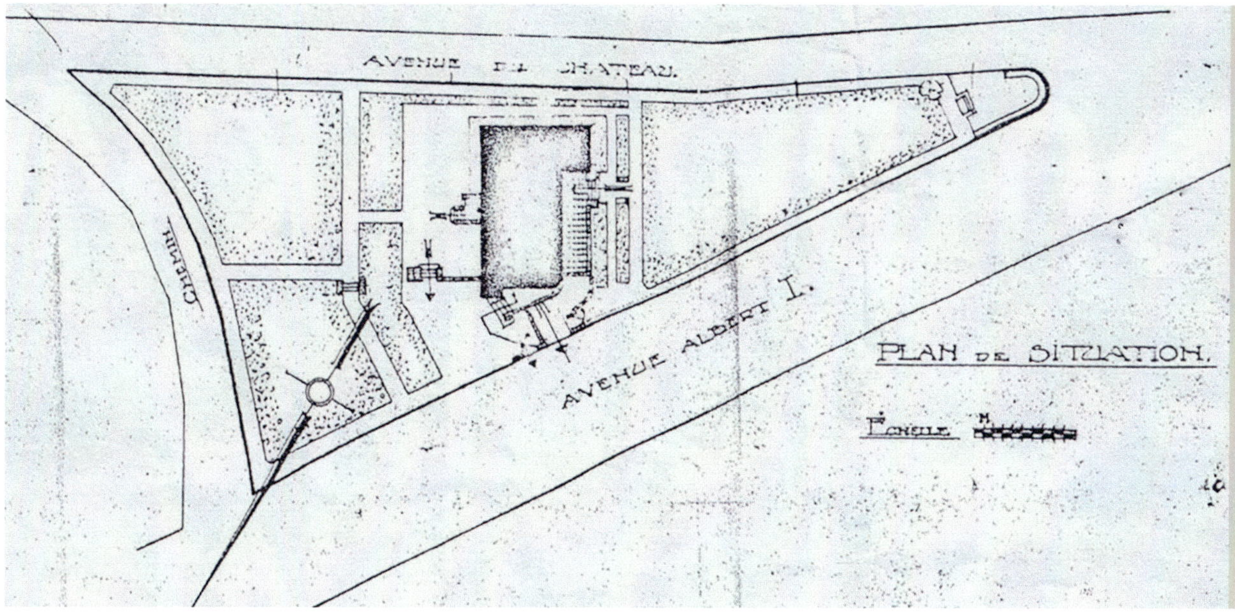

The only historical project drawing of the garden layout, included in a publication in *La Cité* from 1933. The main configuration of the garden, as seen in the historical photographs, is clearly recognisable.

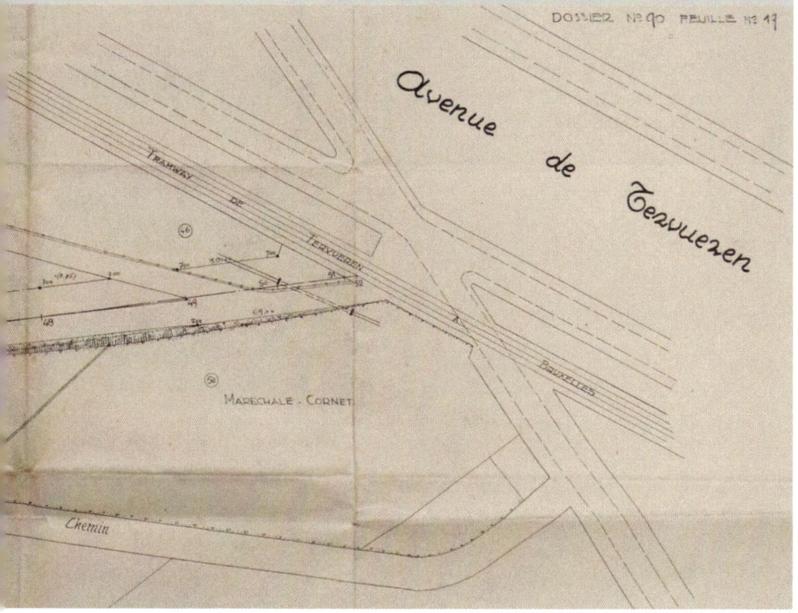

Drone image of the restored garden. The three usage zones are clearly identifiable: the orchard and vegetable garden on one side of the house, and the meadow on the other.

HERITAGE PROTECTION

La Nouvelle Maison was granted comprehensive heritage protection, encompassing both its interior and exterior, by ministerial decree on 9 November 1994. The triangular garden plot consists of three cadastral plots: the smallest central one on which the house is located, flanked by two unbuilt plots. Initially, the historic preservation decree only applied to the central plot: the garden's layout had diverged significantly from its original design, with the topography and functional divisions replaced by a uniform, gently sloping lawn.

It was decided to await the full restoration before revoking the existing partial protection and ultimately safeguarding the entire property in its restored state. Consequently, the previous protection was lifted by ministerial decree on 11 March 2024, and the house, along with the entire garden, was re-protected in its restored condition on the same day.

Terraced lawns around the house divert rainwater away from the building.

Garden walls and terraces serve as starting points for the garden's pathways and structural lines – the meadow side.

The garden terrace at the southern tip of the garden forms a protective prow with a view of Tervurenlaan and the Arboretum in the Sonian Forest. Due to the landscaped elevation difference with the street, one remains invisible to passers-by when seated.

View from the garden terrace towards the house.

The paved paths follow the original historical routes. In the kitchen garden, they are made of compacted locally sourced loam. On the three other sides of the house, they consist of flagstones with irregular wide joints filled with a lean substrate. This substrate supports a variety of extensive vegetation that, without need for maintenance, spontaneously take on different forms depending on the weather, the season, and foot traffic.

THE RESTORATION

CONSERVATION, ECOLOGY, AND BEAUTY

Restoration is a broad term that encompasses various approaches, ranked by international charters as follows, in descending order of preference: conservation, restoration, reconstruction, and renovation. To conserve means to ensure that the condition of an object does not deteriorate, with no loss of material or cohesion; this includes maintenance and minor repairs. Restoration involves improving the condition and appearance of what still exists. Reconstruction refers to the process of rebuilding or recreating something that has been damaged or destroyed, while renovation entails replacing materials and techniques with contemporary alternatives. The restoration of La Nouvelle Maison, like all comprehensive restorations, is a blend of these approaches, with a clear emphasis on conservation. Each of these strategies can only be undertaken after thorough preliminary investigations into the object's original condition, its evolution and the extent of damage. Such investigations provide the foundation for understanding what is necessary and feasible. John Ruskin (1819–1900) was a passionate advocate of conservation:

> Restoration (…) means the most total destruction which a building can suffer: a destruction out of which no remnants can be gathered: a destruction accompanied with false description of the thing destroyed. Do not let us deceive ourselves in this important matter; it is impossible, as impossible as to raise the dead, to restore anything that has ever been great or beautiful in architecture.[35]

After numerous attempts to escape this impossibility, I must concede that there are few examples to the contrary. The demands and agreement with the owners, therefore, centred on salvaging as much authenticity as possible and making the original wholeness, simplicity, and unity visible once more. This theme and ambition have been present from the very beginning, even before the investigations commenced, and it is a long journey. Authenticity pertains to the past, which may seem like a given. However, in the practice of restoration, the authenticity, beauty, and wholeness are initially unknown. At best, they may still be discernible through the mutilations – perhaps not despite but because of the pain of decay. Knowledge is accompanied by prejudices and expectations, and this holds true in the fields of art history and restoration. Yet, any careful restoration can show the artist and the monument, often surprising us by being better or different than anticipated. In this sense, careful restoration is serendipity at work. But any careful restoration will show the author and the monument being surprisingly better or different than anticipated.

Like good design, effective restoration must involve 'listening carefully to what the monument wanted to be' and what it still aspires to be. And then there is another level of acceptance: accepting repair. The way heritage buildings are constructed lends itself to maintenance and local repair. However, today, the necessary resources and expertise have become scarce, making appropriate maintenance and repair less appealing. This situation is exacerbated by perceived quality arguments that favour replacement, waste, and consumption. In short, repair and maintenance have become challenging and are no longer competitive; this has certainly not improved since Ruskin raised his objections in 1849. Protected architectural heritage has been able to endure due to its privileges, but the pressure from broader societal interests has never waned. What is the worth of architectural heritage, and what is the cost of preserving it? Meanwhile, out of necessity, there has been a new turn towards minimising replacement and waste. While the climate was not on Ruskin's mind, he did explicitly consider ecology alongside beauty. Cohesion and interaction are essential for both architectural heritage and ecology alike.

> Composition means, literally and simply, putting several things together so as to make one thing out of them; (...). It is the essence of composition that everything should be in a place, perform an intended part, and act, in that part advantageously for everything that is connected with it. Composition, understood in this pure sense, is the type, in the arts of mankind, of the Providential government of the world.[36]

[35] John Ruskin, 'The Lamp of Memory' in *The Seven Lamps of Architecture*, 1849.

[36] Ruskin, *The Elements of Drawing*, 1857.

The restoration work began in the autumn of 2019.

Ruskin first published this in *Elements of Drawings*, and shortly thereafter in *Modern Painters*, where it plays a key role in the chapter titled 'The Law of Help'. In this chapter, he describes a universal organic principle of necessary interaction, which he refers to as 'creative' because this interaction fosters cohesion. Creativity is not a quality of the author but rather arises from the active interplay between part and whole. The idea that a heritage building is 'impossible to restore' is based on the premise that nothing can enhance the law of help 'at work', including the restorer, if that interaction is already present in the 'wholeness' of the original building. If this is the case, the building cares for itself better than we think we could.

The calmness of cohesion in La Nouvelle Maison is misleading; it appears as if everything speaks for itself and has come together effortlessly. The principle of 'working until everything is where it is supposed to be' is evident in the analysis of both the building itself and the construction records in the library of La Cambre. This is illustrated by the large number of detailed drawings depicting the same elements: brick bonds, windows, wrought ironwork, technical ducts, and the organisation of the water supply and drainage infrastructure, as well as heating pipes and rainwater drains. All these technical aspects can only be freed from disruptive 'unfortunateness' if they do not appear to be coincidental due to a lack of foresight. Design requirements continuously flow back and forth between the part and the whole.

This two-way flow was fully developed in van de Velde's practice at the time he designed La Nouvelle Maison. His experience with wooden prefabrication[37] and the development of new technologies led to an integrated design method, blurring the boundary between structural work and finishing. Techniques needed to be reconciled with the overall design and find their place in the building's shell. Compared to his earlier oeuvre, La Nouvelle Maison marked a period in which industrial materials significantly influenced the design. This applies to the exposed brick,[38] modulated for use in windowsills, door sills, capstones, steps, lintels, and so on, as well as to the exposed concrete, standard steel window profiles, parapets made from standard plumbing pipes, and connectors. In the evolution of the planning process, the visibility of structural and standard materials within the compositions presents an additional design challenge compared to structural elements with finishing coats.

Many have sought to understand the role of the interaction between part and whole, viewing it as the essence of life and art. For Goethe (1749–1832)[39], as well as for Christopher Alexander (1936–2022)[40] 200 years later, that interaction arises from consistent action in creating the part. This idea of local action at the part level is particularly valuable in conservation and restoration. However, in what direction does the action go when multiple approaches are possible?

Patrick Geddes (1854–1932), often regarded as the modern father of the GLOCAL sustainability concept, described the method of intervening in an existing context as 'conservative surgery'. This method, akin to the steps in van de Velde's *méthode de la beauté*, is free from aesthetic biases and is rooted in the essence of GLOCAL thinking: 'think globally, act locally'. This means considering what the part signifies within the whole and acting accordingly. It invites us to understand how the part contributes to the whole, acting 'advantageously for everything that is connected with it' (Ruskin).

If there is a way to escape the impossibility of restoration (cf. Ruskin), it lies in the practice of GLOCAL, where it is not uncommon for the conclusion to be to do nothing. This is not self-evident, as aesthetic demands and consumerism often burden the restorer with the fear of falling short. To counter this, I draw on the thoughts of Karl Popper, who argues that restoring as minimally as possible does matter and can have a global impact, provided it is done consistently and skilfully.

> **I do not suggest that piecemeal engineering cannot be bold, or that it must be confined to 'smallish' problems. But I think that the degree of complication which we can tackle is governed by the degree of our experience gained in conscious and systematic piecemeal engineering.[41]**

It is fascinating to see how la *méthode de la beauté* parallels 'piecemeal engineering' in many ways. If we replace 'bold' with *beauté*, Karl Popper's statement aligns with van de Velde's 'stages of beauty'. 'Conscious and systematic' corresponds to 'rational and neutral', while 'degree of experience' refers to perfection.

37 In the decade leading up to the construction of La Nouvelle Maison, van de Velde completed several projects in the Netherlands involving prefabricated, standardised, and modular timber construction. His own house, De Tent, in Wassenaar is certainly not unique in that regard. By designing for prefabrication, his relationship with production processes changed in the run-up to the Tervuren house.

38 In the preceding decade, van de Velde did design façades featuring exposed brick; however, the details – such as capstones, windowsills, and steps – were executed in other materials. Shortly after La Nouvelle Maison, he went on to design the von Schinckel-van de Velde house in Hamburg, the Kröller-Müller house in Wassenaar, the Fondation M.J. Heinemann in Hanover, and the Hôtel Wolfers in Brussels. Even more radically honest in its use of standard materials is the G. Cohen textile factory in Ninove, which dates like La Nouvelle Maison from 1928.

39 John Ruskin's 'law of help' aligns with J.W. von Goethe's dynamic perspective on the interaction between part and whole. He states: 'Every creature is its own reason to be. All its parts have a direct effect on one another, a relationship to one another, thereby constantly renewing the circle of life'. Goethe, *Scientific Studies*, ed. and trans. Douglas Miller (Princeton: Princeton University Press, 1995), p. 121. And: 'If we would seek comfort in the whole, we must learn to discover the whole in the smallest part.'

40 For Christopher Alexander, wholeness is a quality that emerges rather than one that is designed. This perspective resonates with van de Velde's concept of '*la ligne*', which is free from rigid biases and formalistic thinking. Form develops naturally, and cohesion is achieved through consistent actions, executed with care and the appropriate tools. For Alexander, cohesion is also structurally related ('recursive structure') facilitated by active feedback loops between the parts and the whole, much like Goethe's understanding. Alexander's efforts to comprehend and articulate wholeness span over thirty years, evolving from *Nature of Order* to *The Battle for the Life and Beauty of the Earth*.

41 Karl Popper, in *The Open Society and its Enemies*, vol. I, *The Spell of Plato*, 1952. The full name of the concept is 'piecemeal social engineering', which stands in contrast to utopian ideals.

Popper approached this from a societal perspective, rather than focusing on beauty. However, the similarity is not surprising; the continuity between society and art was also recognised by those thinkers who inspired van de Velde, such as Goethe, Ruskin, Schopenhauer, and Nietzsche.

Restoration is a highly dynamic activity involving constant zooming in and out. The question of whether something is necessary always hinges on examining the whole. Does damage to a part pose a threat to the integrity of the whole? 'Threat' should be understood in functional terms. Does the part still function 'advantageously for everything that is connected with it' – technically and practically, as well as in the interplay that van de Velde refers to as *la ligne*?

A concrete example is façade cleaning. The key is to determine to what extent and where exactly the dirt obscures the legibility of the mass. It is helpful to revisit the big picture: 'architecture reduced to masses, a dialogue of solids and voids; an architecture deeply rooted in the ground, as if it were the very fruit of it'. The challenge in restoration is to strike a balance between 'not losing the sand-coating' and 'mitigating local dirt build-up'.[42]

Other examples include local repairs to the concrete cornice, reusing and repairing broken marble slabs, and accepting the locally missing pieces from the wooden shutters as long as they continue to function.

It is clear that in an environment where perfection is demanded and feigned from everything and everyone, a shift towards neutral and observant acceptance of visible repairs is necessary. In my experience, 'conscious and systematic piecemeal engineering' does not disturb the balance of wholeness, greatness, and beauty. Just as van de Velde advocated 125 years ago a new aesthetic that was subordinate to reason and function, thereby laying the foundation for the Bauhaus, so too is restoration, and, by extension, our approach to everything we possess, an exercise in the subservient aesthetics of consistent and functional restoration.

PRELIMINARY INVESTIGATIONS

What follows does not so much describe the results of the preliminary investigations but rather the method and its importance and application for the restoration. As with rational design and *la méthode de la beauté*, the point to which the preliminary investigations lead is not the final result, but it is indeed determining.

A Dialectic Approach

Preliminary investigations occur in parallel and often in contradiction. The aim is not to immediately reach consensus but to enter the project and implementation phase with a clear understanding of certainties and uncertainties.

Each preliminary study first arrives at a conclusion separately, based on its specific scientific methods and data. Once all conclusions have been gathered, the restoration architect prepares a report detailing the contradictions and gaps among the preliminary investigations and organises a meeting to discuss these discrepancies, with each investigation team outlining its margins of interpretation. An assessment is made as to whether additional investigations or checks are necessary in the individual research areas. Each researcher thus remains neutral and comfortable within their specific field of investigation. As long as everyone proceeds competently, consistently, and conscientiously, there are no incorrect conclusions, regardless of the remaining contradictions. If contradictions persist even after additional investigations, the final verdict remains inconclusive, and it is determined where attention should be focused during the restoration to ultimately eliminate the contradiction.

With a clear overview of certainties, unresolved issues, and gaps, the project plan is developed, and the work is outlined. Typically, there is an assumption for each unresolved issue that underpins the specification text, along with an alternative for which price agreements have already been established in the bids. In planning the work, the search for answers is incorporated at an early stage.

The Original Construction Plans

In the Fonds van de Velde at La Cambre, there exists a collection of 122 documents from Henry van de Velde, relating to the construction of La Nouvelle Maison. Some documents, such as the work notebook containing construction site notes and calculations, comprise as many as 50 pages. There are also large plans that contain useful information, including details on the

[42] There were precedents involving other buildings where the Belvedere stone had been cleaned too aggressively, resulting in façades that appeared rustic rather than exuding a sense of mass. The façade of La Nouvelle Maison was initially cleaned using saturated steam on a global scale, a technique effective only for removing light dirt. More aggressive local cleaning led to the loss of sand and exposed the yellow core beneath. The remaining disruptive pollution consisted of black dirt trapped in calcite and sulphate crusts on the joints, creating an unsightly patina of vertical bands where rain had been most prominent. This phenomenon is normal; the shape and orientation of a façade influence where it absorbs and releases water, with the black zones indicating areas where water seeps out. Because this type of contamination is stubborn, and a global approach could further damage the sand, it was decided to locally mitigate the issue by scrubbing the joints with a narrow metal brush until their grey value matched that of the stone.

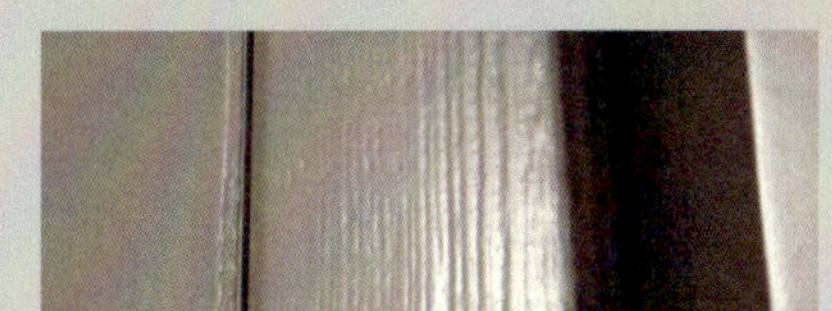

Restoration, and, more broadly, caring for everything we possess, is an exercise in a humble aesthetic of consistent and functional repair: Does the element still function, 'advantageously for everything that is connected with it'? (Ruskin).

reverse. To protect these documents while ensuring they remain accessible for in-depth research, they were first digitised and assigned a unique ID. Not all documents are dated, but it was possible to organise the key documents chronologically based on the consistent changes in content.

Building History Research

This research describes the historical facts surrounding the building, the context of its construction, relevant information during the construction process, and the changes made over the years.

Henry van de Velde lived in La Nouvelle Maison from 1928 to 1947. He was married to Maria Sèthe (1867–1943), and they had five children: Nele (1897–1965), Lene (1899–1935), Anne (1901–45), and twins Thylla (1904–55) and Thyl (1904–80). Lene and Anne were already married when the house was completed, and Thylla and Thyl married within a year of moving in. Only Nele continued to live there, unmarried. To provide her with her own spacious living unit, van de Velde created connections between all the rooms on the first storey on the southwest side. This adaptation was part of the reference condition for the restoration.

Later, during or after WWII, van de Velde also altered the colour scheme. The circumstances and reasons for this change are not known. The dark green exterior joinery was transformed to off-white. Changes were also made to the interior colours, although these were less dramatic. The initial colour scheme (with green windows) became the reference condition for the restoration.

Normalised Plans

Drawings reflect the maker's thinking; normalised measurements or plans are a way to retain that original thinking after the contingencies of execution. Normalised plans of architectural heritage sites provide continuity to historical documents.
Just as spatial continuity in architecture aids in understanding spatial cohesion, so too does continuity in plans help to convey relevant information about the authentic composition for future generations.

At the foundation of a design is a concept, translated into manufacturable geometry in drawings. The design process and implementation plans are a thoughtful continuation of this. During execution, tolerances – i.e. margins of error – are traditionally allowed, accounting for the difference between actual and nominal dimensions.

A wall drawn straight is always curved in reality; a floor is never completely horizontal. A right angle is rarely built at a perfect 90 degrees. A window opening in a building's shell may differ from left to right. Within tolerance limits, this rarely poses a practical problem, as good detail work accommodates such variations. Skilled builders ensure that any mistakes remain inconspicuous or do not cause irritation by making irregularities appear regular.

To measure is to interpret an existing state with the aim of creating a meaningful summary of it. Similarly, a transcription of a musical performance serves as a meaningful summary, while a recording does not. Neither is a scan or photogrammetry of a building a meaningful summary. A heritage building survey should provide insight into all aspects of the structure, including both formal and technical elements. Construction and penetrating detail work must be recorded to interpret the surface, behaviour, and damage, as well as to predict the effects of restoration interventions.

In the case of a heritage building, the thought processes and continued reflection of the creators are integral to its meaning. When measuring such a building, the aim is to distinguish between this original thinking and any other significant historical facts related to the object. By comparing available records and documents of the original thinking (such as implementation plans) with the existing state, it is possible to identify differences and determine their significance. Meaningful differences for restoration might include a desired remodelling (as van de Velde did with the first storey), a deflection, subsidence, etc. Anything that falls outside the tolerances of execution may already hold significance in recording the original thought.

For a normalised survey, the plans originally used for implementation are compared with the dimensions of the existing condition. Afterwards, all differences that fall within the tolerances are neutralised. Larger deviations are considered 'possibly intended' and must be interpreted. The tolerances applicable to the general plans at a 1:50 scale of La Nouvelle

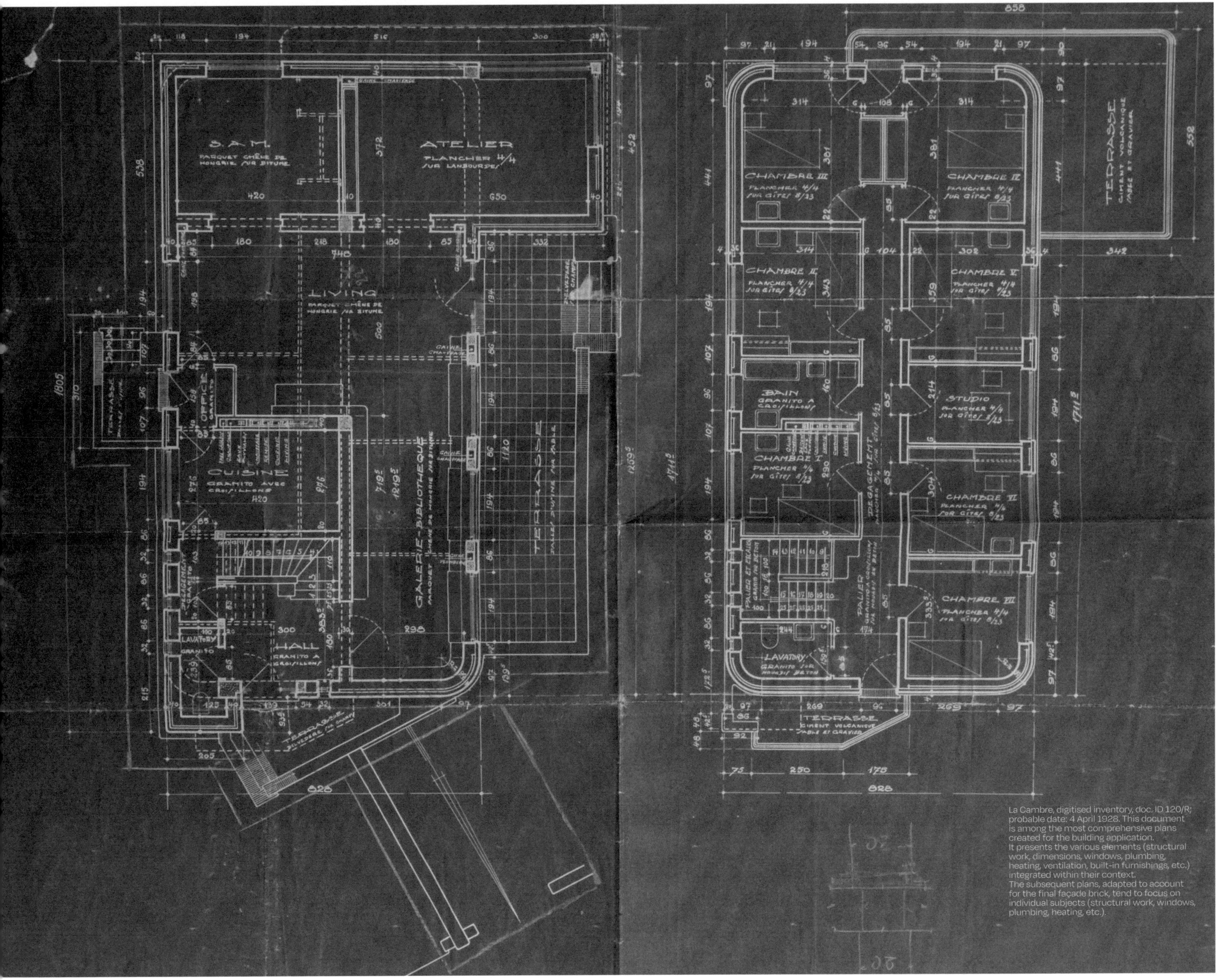

La Cambre, digitised inventory, doc. ID 120/R; probable date: 4 April 1928. This document is among the most comprehensive plans created for the building application. It presents the various elements (structural work, dimensions, windows, plumbing, heating, ventilation, built-in furnishings, etc.) integrated within their context. The subsequent plans, adapted to account for the final façade brick, tend to focus on individual subjects (structural work, windows, plumbing, heating, etc.).

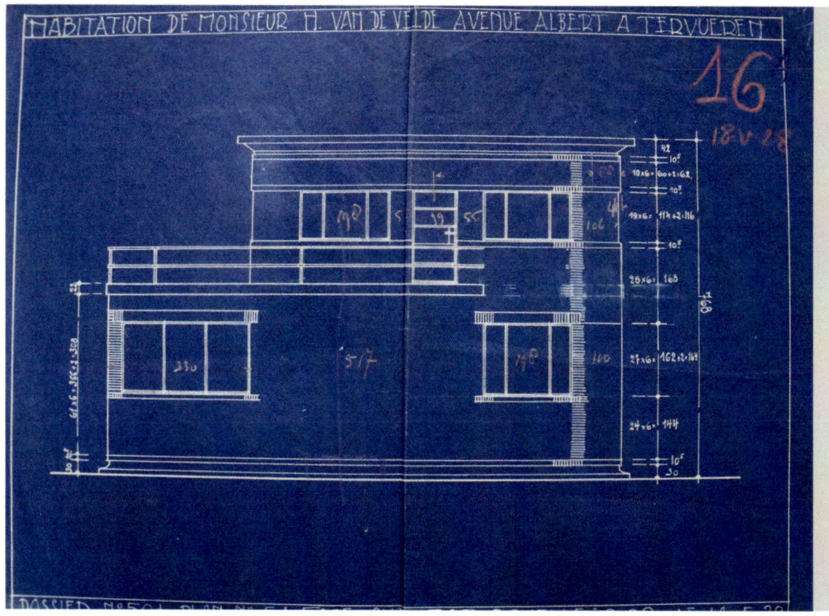

La Cambre, digitised inventory, doc. ID 001/R; date: 18 May 1928. This plan also depicts the state of affairs prior to the first major modification, which involved adding a full basement to the house.

La Cambre, digitised inventory, doc. ID 110/R; date after June 1928. Purchase order of the wooden floor beams for the first storey.

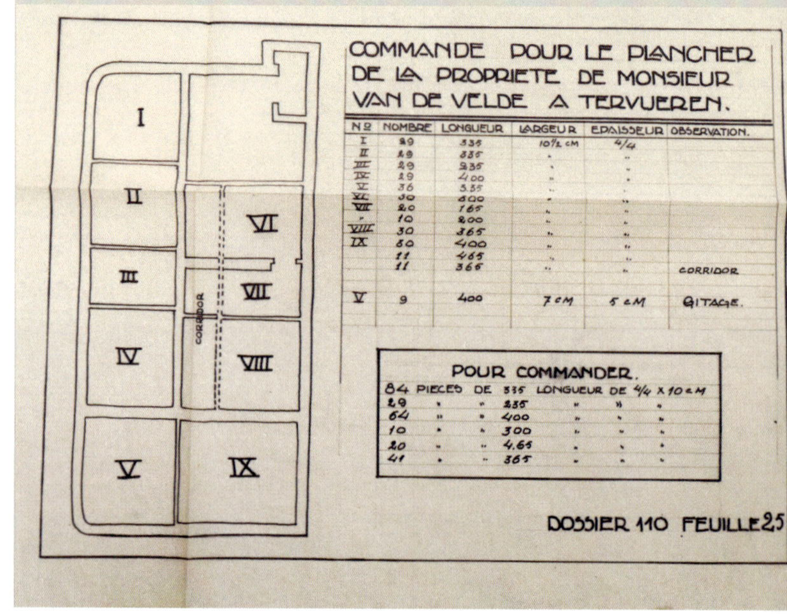

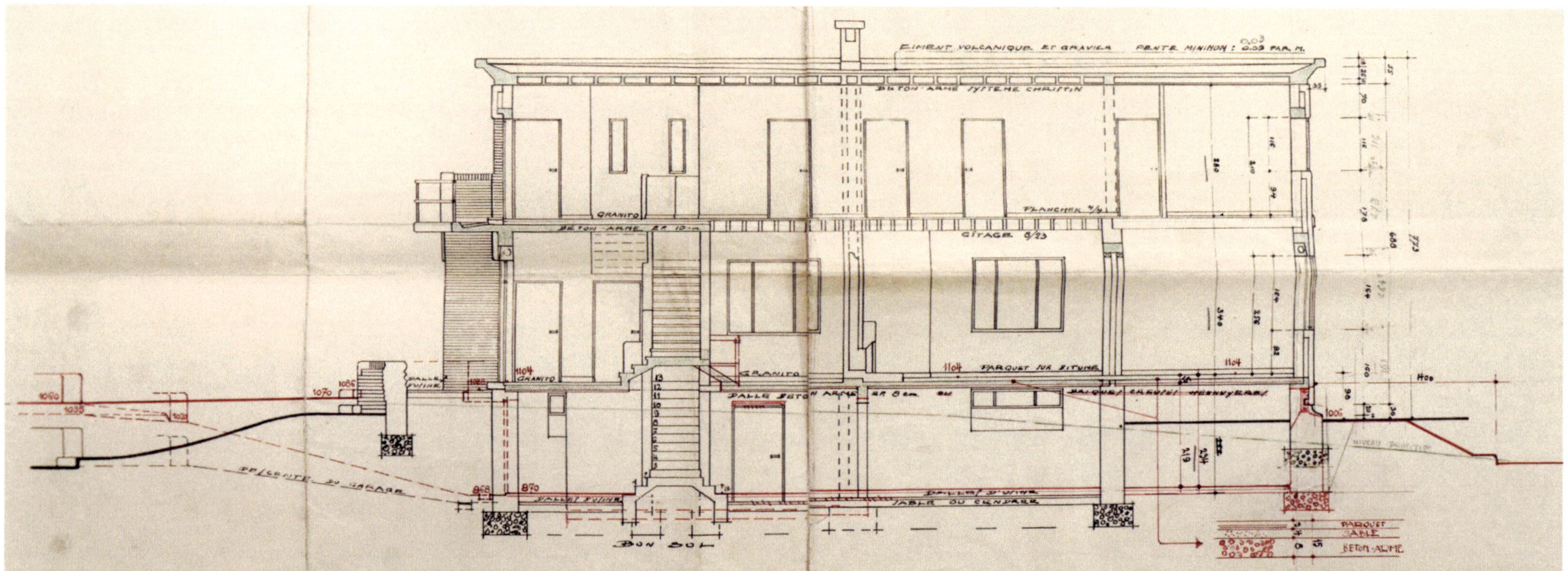

La Cambre, digitised inventory, doc. ID 017/R; date: 20/04/1928. This plan shows the modifications – marked in red – to the planning drawings, following the topographical survey of the site and the final determination of the level of the new Albertlaan, which would be built at a higher elevation.

La Cambre, digitised inventory, doc. ID 057/R; date after June 1928. Detailed drawing of the brick bonds for the concave plinth.

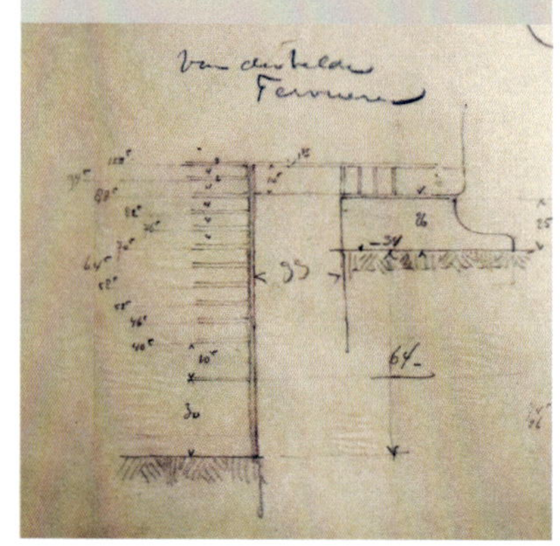

La Cambre, digitised inventory, doc. ID 030/R; date unknown. Full-scale detail drawing of the double steel profile above the living area.

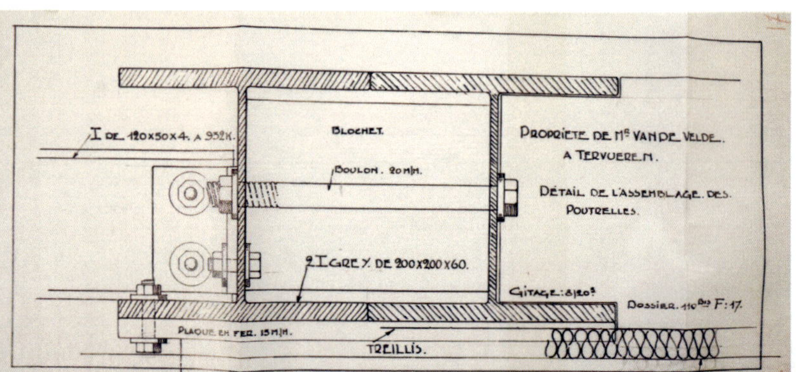

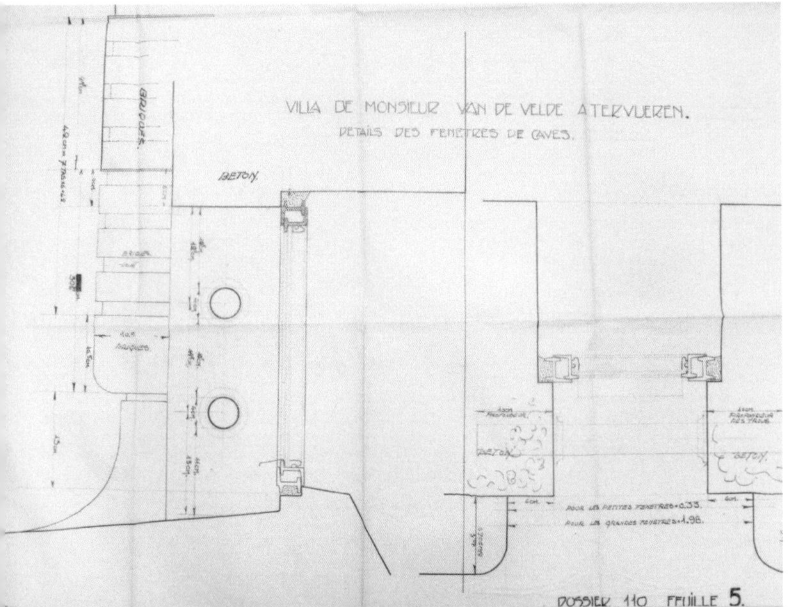

La Cambre, digitised inventory, doc. ID 038/R; date after June 1928. Full-scale detail drawing of the house's base and basement window.

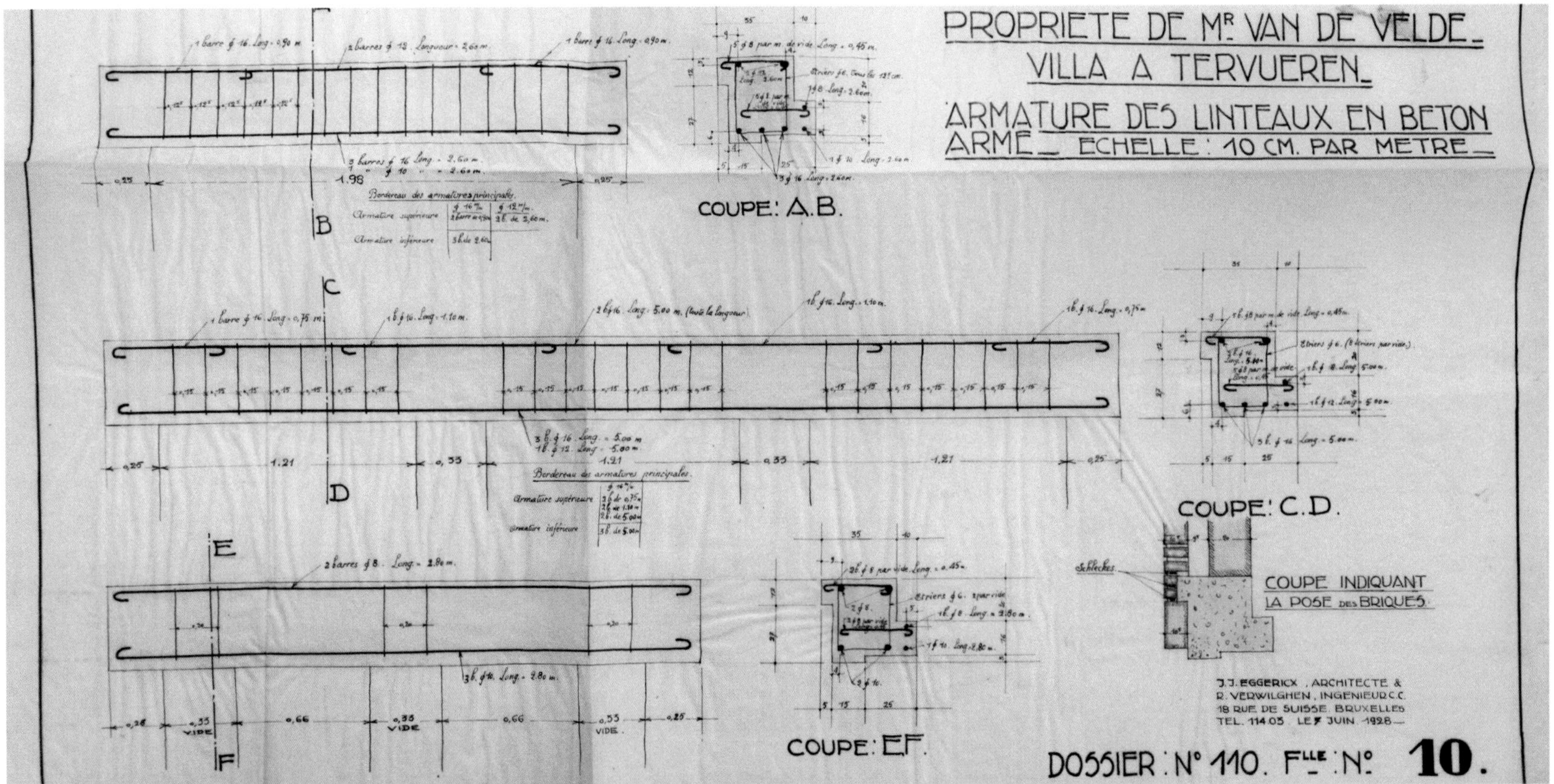

La Cambre, digitised inventory, doc. ID 045/R; date after June 1928. Detailed drawing of the concrete façade lintels above the basement windows.

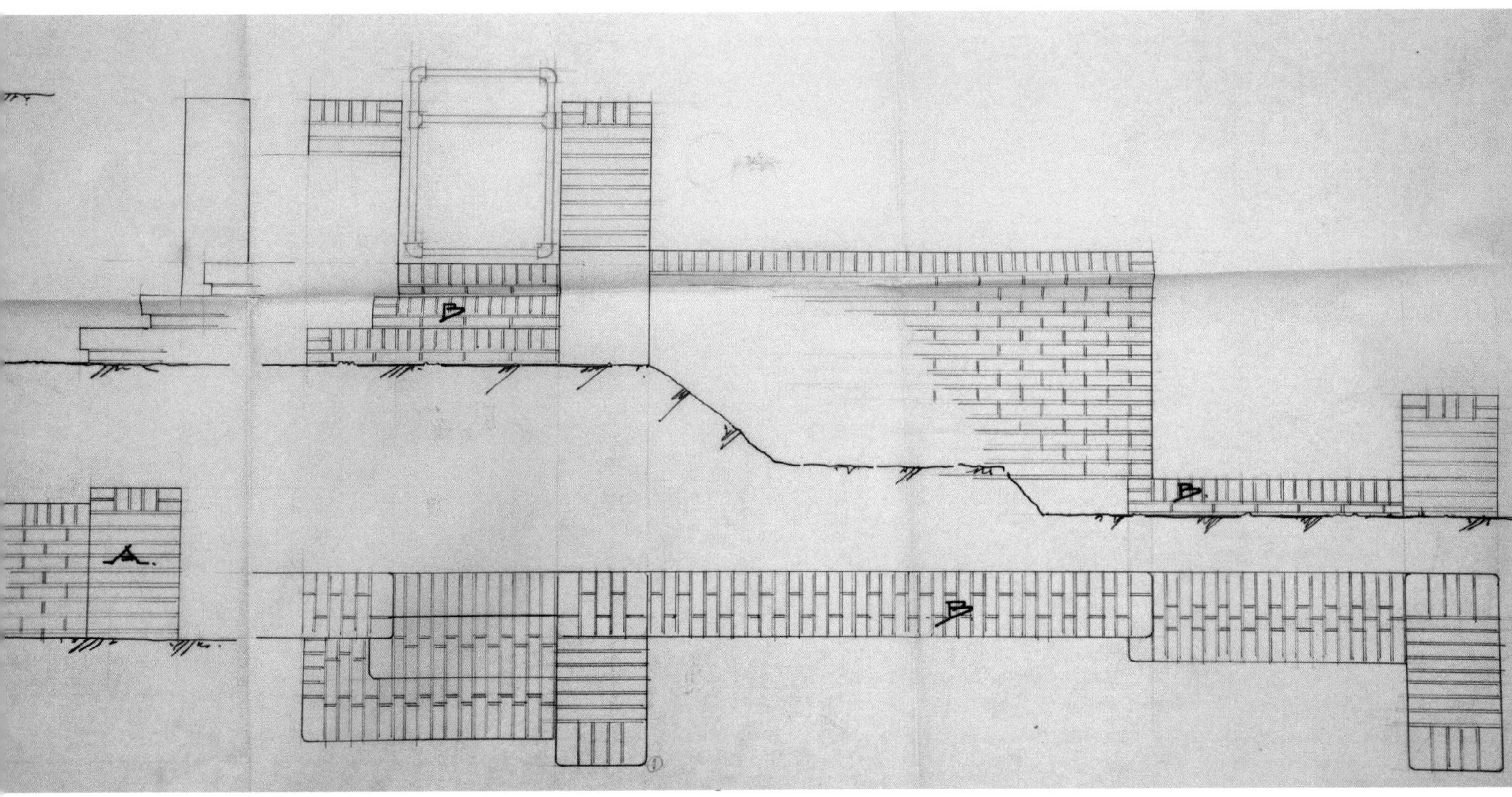

La Cambre, digitised inventory, doc. ID 042/R; date after June 1928. Detailed drawing of the brick bonds for the garden walls.

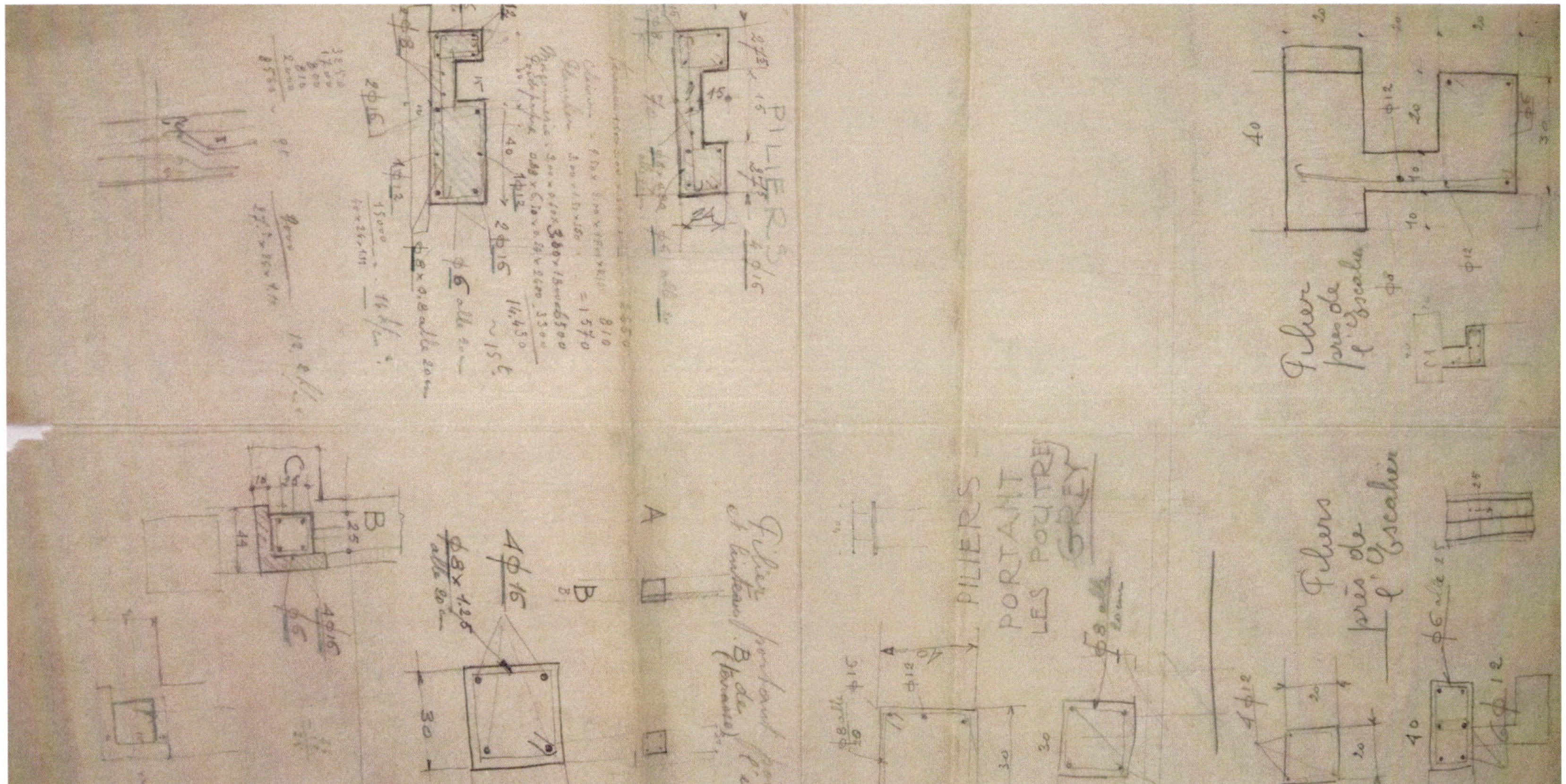

La Cambre, digitised inventory, doc. ID 100/R; date after June 1928. Handwritten instructions and details can be found on the reverse side of numerous documents, such as here for the reinforced concrete foundation columns.

La Cambre, digitised inventory, doc. ID 111/R; date after June 1928. Detailed drawing of the parapets of the first-storey terraces.

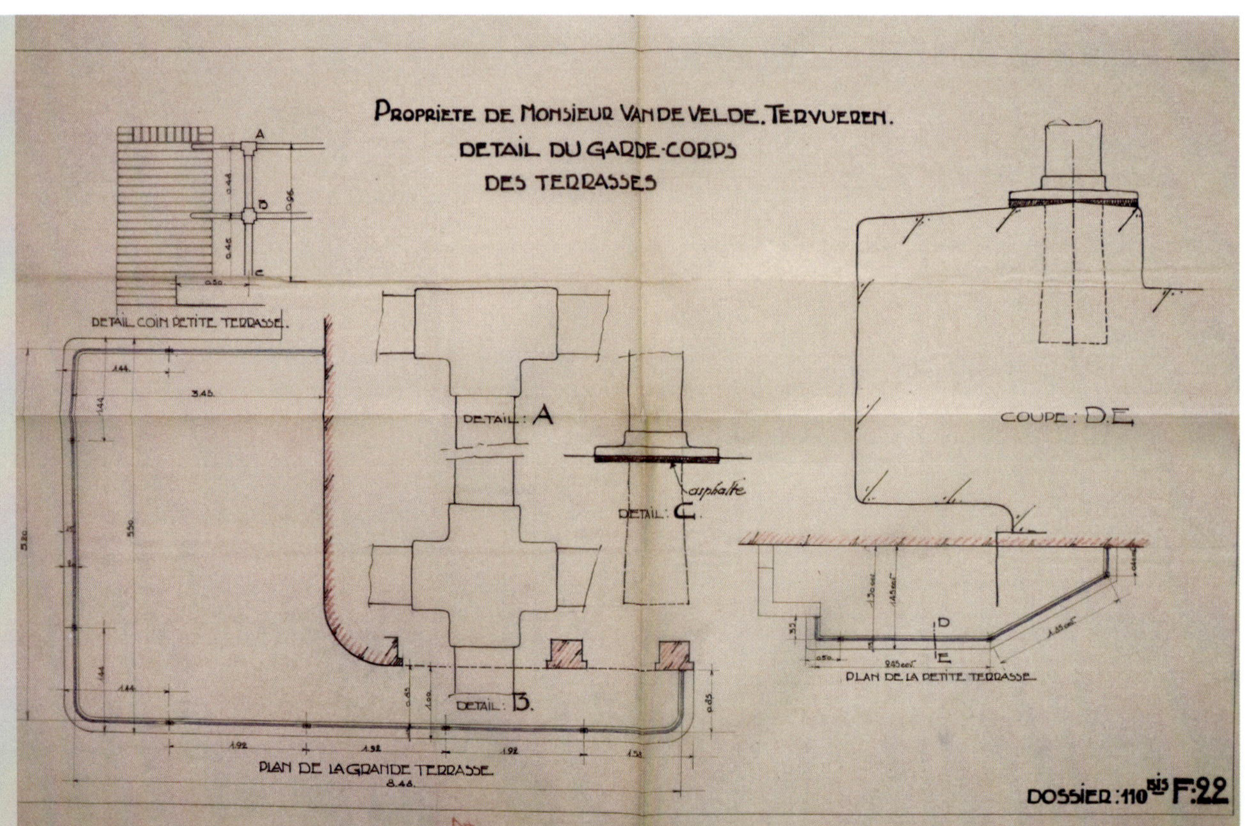

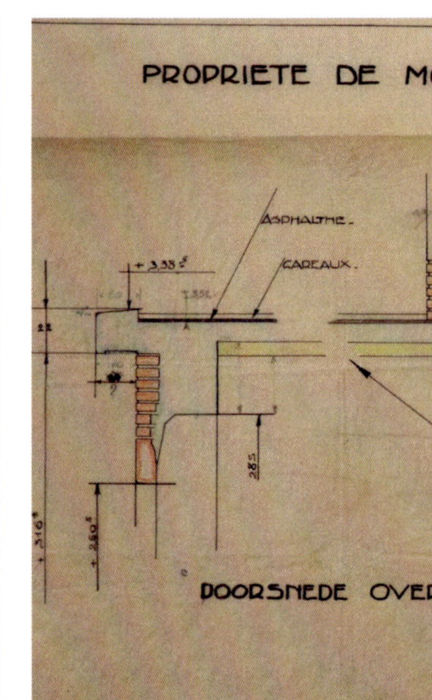

La Cambre, digitised inventory, doc. ID 041/R; date after June 1928. Early detail drawing for the wrought iron work of the garden gates.

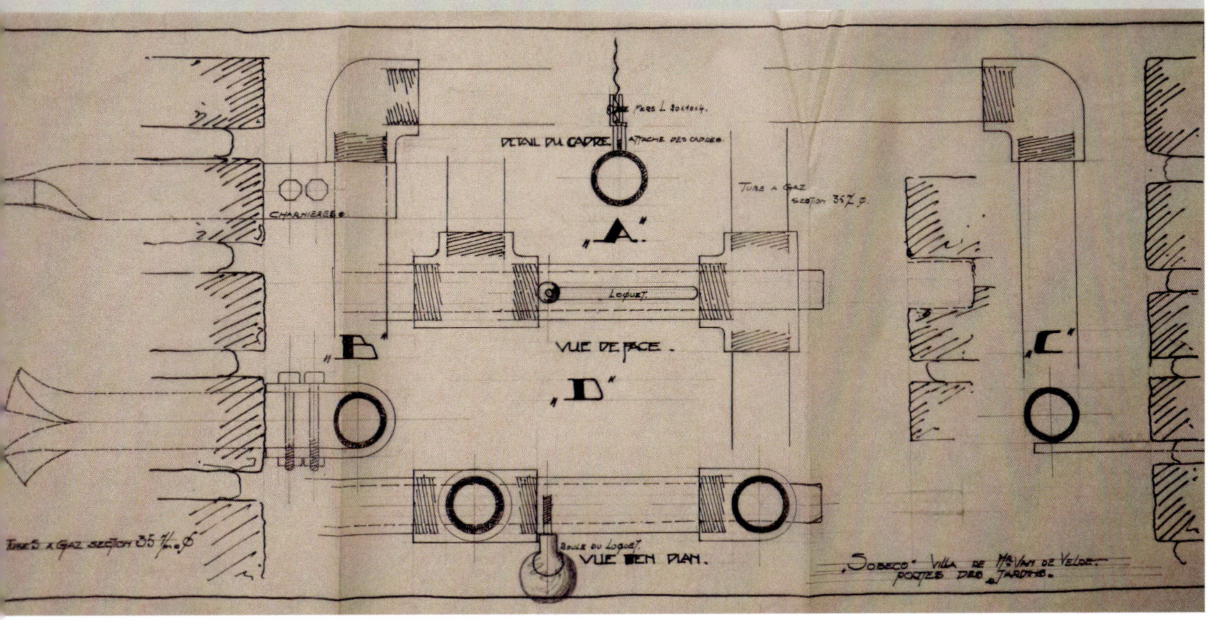

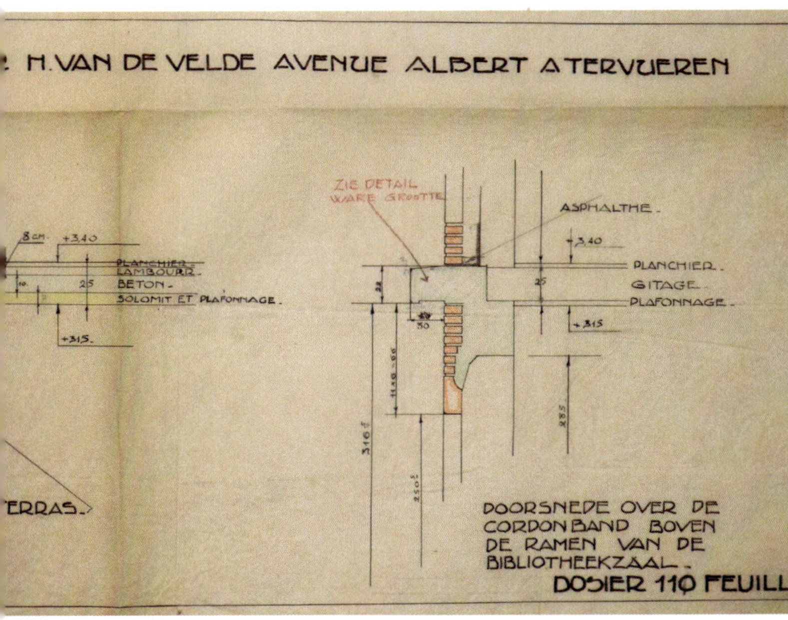

La Cambre, digitised inventory, doc. ID 046/R; date after June 1928. Technical cross-sections of the concrete lintels above the ground-floor windows and the concrete slab above the studio. It is shown that this concrete slab had to be insulated on the underside with 7 cm of 'Solomit', an insulation material made of compressed and bound reeds. This was verified during preliminary investigations, confirming that this insulation was indeed applied.

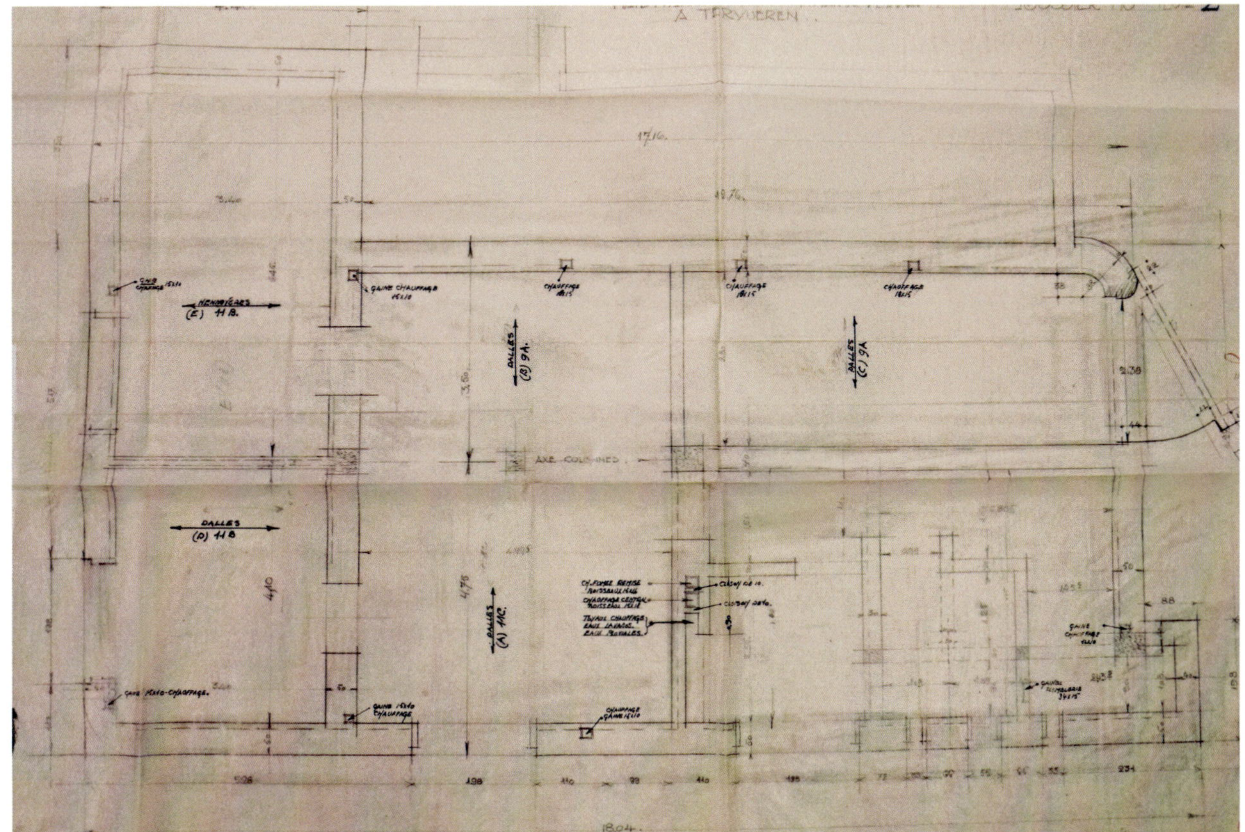

La Cambre, digitised inventory, doc. ID 055/R en 062/R; date after June 1928.
The technical ducts had, and still have, specific purposes: heating, plumbing, etc.

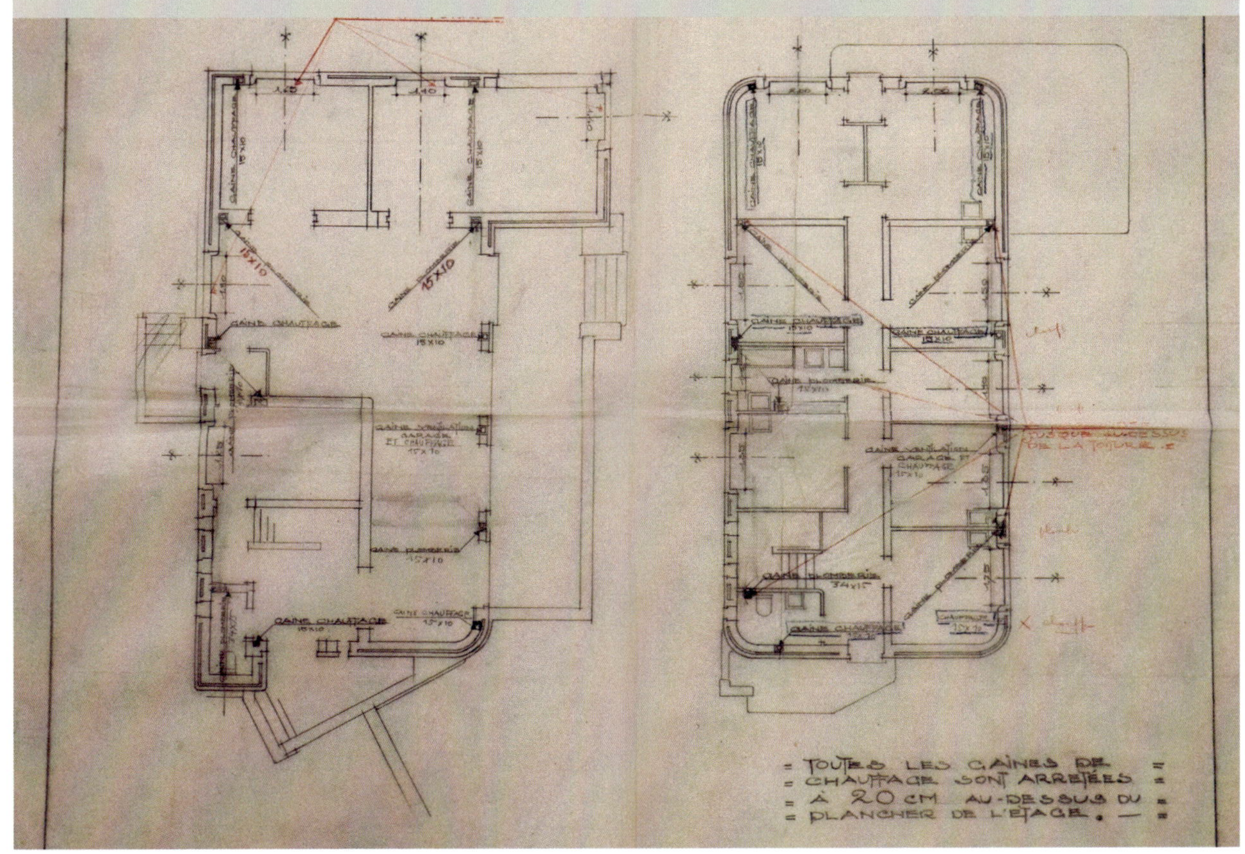

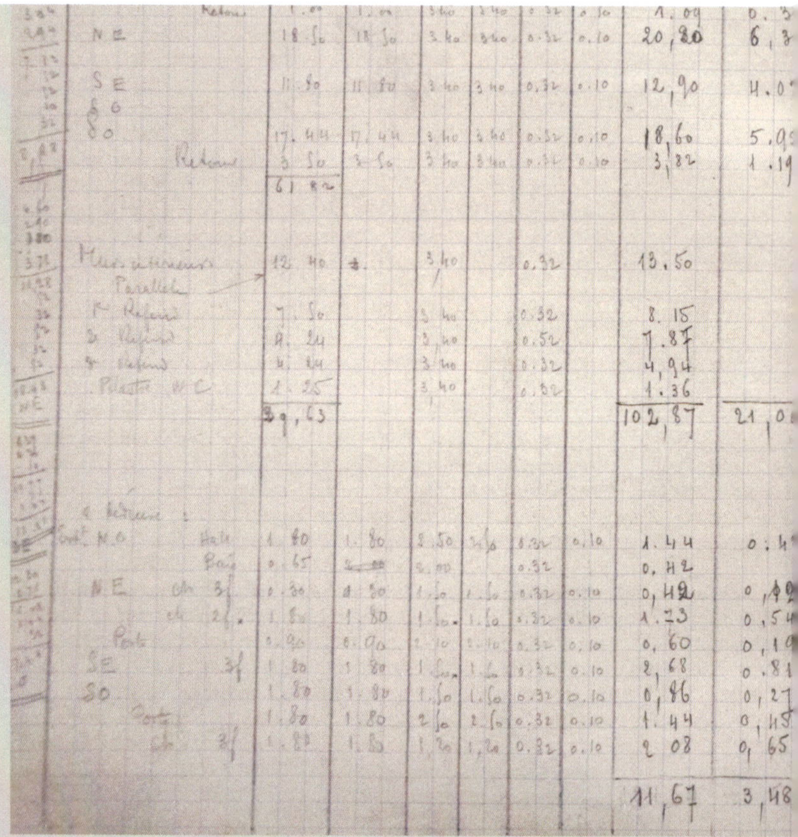

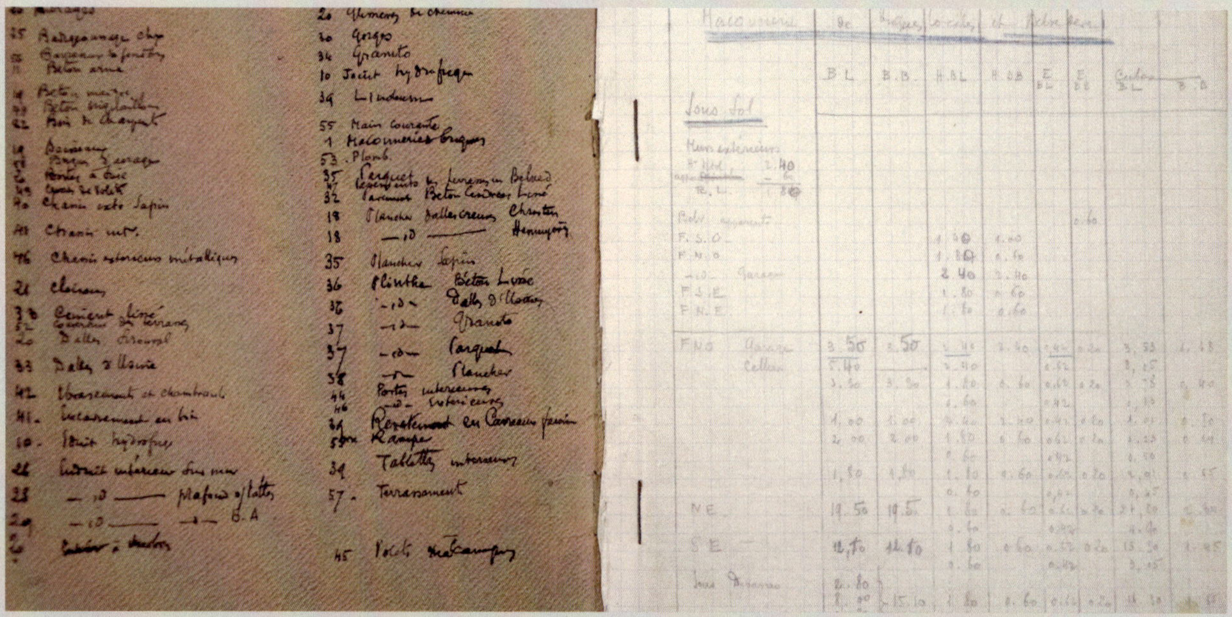

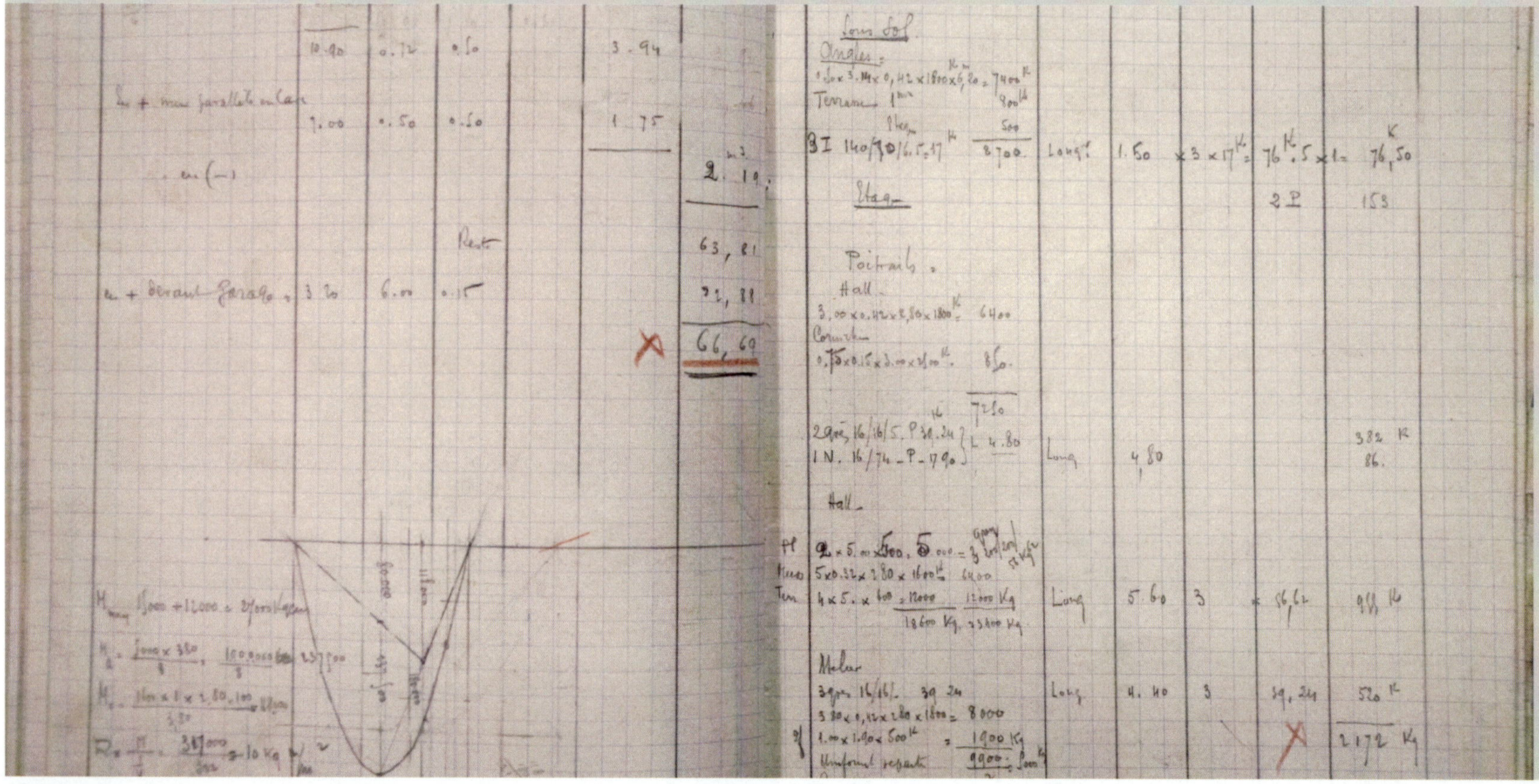

La Cambre, digitised inventory, doc. ID 122/P; date during construction. The brown notebook in the archive contains a wealth of useful technical, qualitative, and quantitative information about La Nouvelle Maison: calculations of quantities, structural calculations, material specifications, agreements, modifications, etc. Alongside the plans, it provides a clear picture of the ongoing design process in which detailing – on account of the honest and visible use of materials and integrated techniques – is continuously refined.

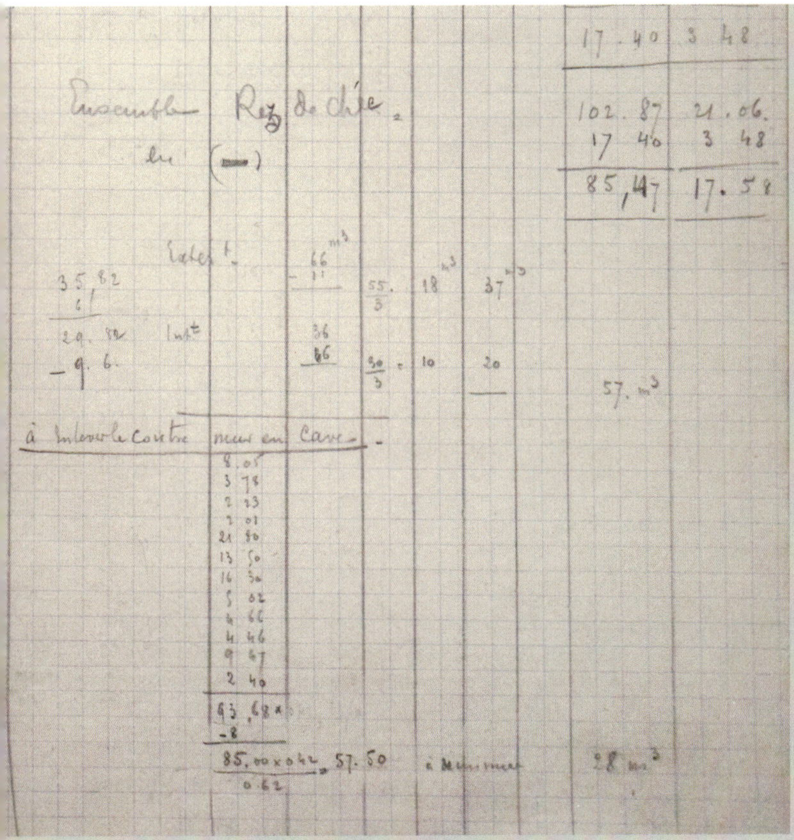
Ensemble Rez de chée
17. 40 3 48
102. 87 21. 06.
17 40 3 48
85,47 17. 58
57. m3
28 m3

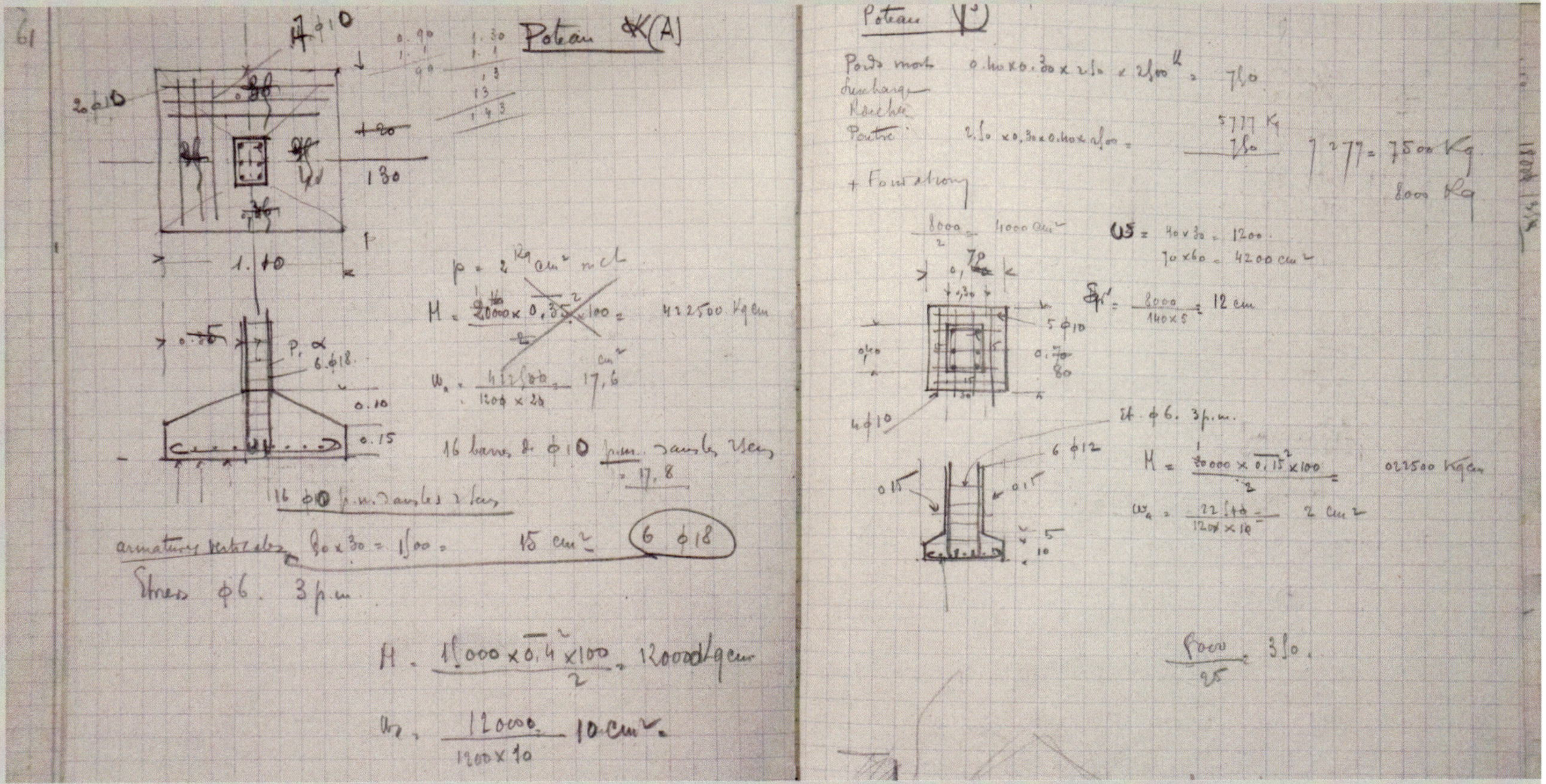
Poteau (A)
16 barres de ϕ10
armatures verticales 30 x 50 = 1500 = 15 cm² 6 ϕ18
Etriers ϕ6. 3 p.m.
M = 1000 x 0.4² x 100 / 2 = 12000 kgcm
W = 12000 / 1200 x 10 = 10 cm²
Poteau
Poids mort
Fondations
5 ϕ10
6 ϕ12
4 ϕ10

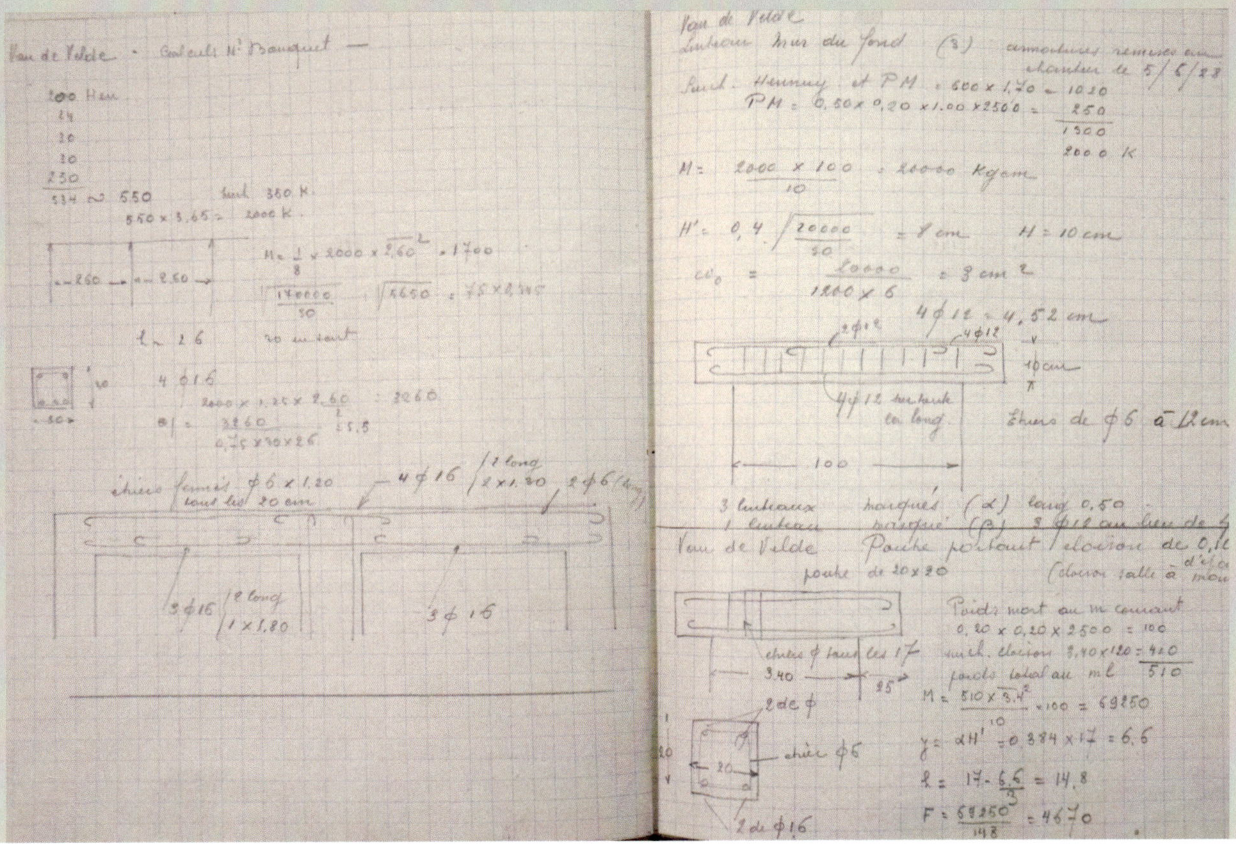
Van de Velde - Calculs Mr Banquet -
4 ϕ16
3 ϕ16
Van de Velde
Linteau mur du fond
M = 2000 x 100 / 10 = 20000 kgcm
4 ϕ12 = 4,52 cm
Etriers de ϕ6 à 12 cm
Van de Velde Poutre portant cloison de 0,10
poutre de 20x20
Poids mort au m courant
2 de ϕ
2 de ϕ16

Maison are 3 cm for local individual measures and 6 cm for global measures.[43] The plans of the existing condition represent the normalised survey; they include drawings at various scales.

It is often said that 'better is the enemy of good'. This is a useful perspective in restoration, particularly when it comes to measuring. Indicating dimensions on restoration drawings differs from its application in new construction. In restoration, the existing condition serves as the starting point, and everything is measured from that baseline. If sporadic measurements of existing states are reported, they are informal and not binding. With every local intervention or execution, measurements should be taken again, as this creates a binding record and aids in visualising, thinking through, and anticipating the work. Restoration is inherently glocal, which presupposes that the details adapt to local conditions.[44]

When dimensions are missing on printed documents, it is not a problem, provided that the scale of the document is chosen so that measuring from it keeps sizes within the limits of tolerances. For example, on a 1:50 document, one can measure to half a millimetre, which corresponds to 2.5 cm in the real world. This is less than 3 cm, the maximum local deviation allowed between reality and normalised measurement. For precise information on normalised measurements, digital vectorised files are available, allowing for measurements with the greatest accuracy if needed.

Stratigraphy

Historic paint analysis – stratigraphy, or the description of layers – examines the evolution of surface finishes on the support. The aim is to determine the colour, gloss value, and binder of each layer. These factors are important not only for understanding how the surface used to look, but also for determining appropriate restoration techniques. For example, this analysis helps establish whether layers should be removed mechanically or chemically, or, if removal is not advisable, to identify the binder for new layers. Stratigraphy provides information about the sequence of finishes at a specific location, rather than their dating. Relative dating, and if possible, absolute dating, is achieved by examining the interfaces between adjacent layers or by cross-referencing with documentation or historical iconography.

Examples in La Nouvelle Maison of information that extends beyond aesthetics include the original finish of the basement walls with lime paint, which contributed to the house's winter inertia and dry cooling capacity. Only the kitchen, bathroom, and lavatory were painted with waterproof paint. All other rooms were finished with lime-based distemper, which enhances the hygrothermal inertia and comfort of the living spaces.

Disassembly Work

The preliminary investigations described above were used to determine what was definitively not original and which non-original elements obscured the extent of the damage. Such additions were removed after authorisation from the heritage authority, including the kitchen, lavatory, and the added flooring on the first storey. Concurrently, an inventory of the original power conduits was conducted, and new wires were run through these conduits during the restoration.

Disassembly is akin to stratigraphy; it reveals the historical layers of the building, serving as the telling material memory of the heritage structure.

Normalised Plans of the Original State

Based on the information provided by previous preliminary investigations and the normalised survey, it is possible to create detailed as-built drawings of the probable original condition. These drawings serve as an important reference document for potential restitutions (reconstructions of lost elements). I emphasise 'potential' restitutions, as restitution remains a choice that must be justified, not an obligation. As-built drawings should not be confused with the reference condition prior to restoration, which may include historical alterations that are preserved.

They offer an opportunity to gain insight – a literal 'rendering visible' – into the original composition, which may have lost cohesion and self-evidence through alterations. A restoration allows monuments to speak for their authentic selves without becoming a caricature of what we perceive they once were. In other words, restoration does not aim to recreate an unadulterated original state.

[43] 6 cm is significant for brick architecture, in the sense that it is half the width of the header of a façade brick plus the joint, rounded up to the nearest centimetre. The exact measurement is secondary to the number of bricks or headers.

[44] A concrete example of subordination of the local to the global in the restoration process was the reconstruction of a section of the low wall along the large western terrace, which had become uneven and frost-damaged due to water infiltration. In the first reconstruction, the new courses were laid straight and horizontal, which highlighted the discrepancies in the existing structure. In the second attempt, the existing condition served as the starting point, and the reconstruction was executed in a 'subsequent' manner – sufficiently curved to appear straight. In a world where everything is dictated by abstract, virtual perfection, adopting an empathetic and tolerant approach is a challenging endeavour.

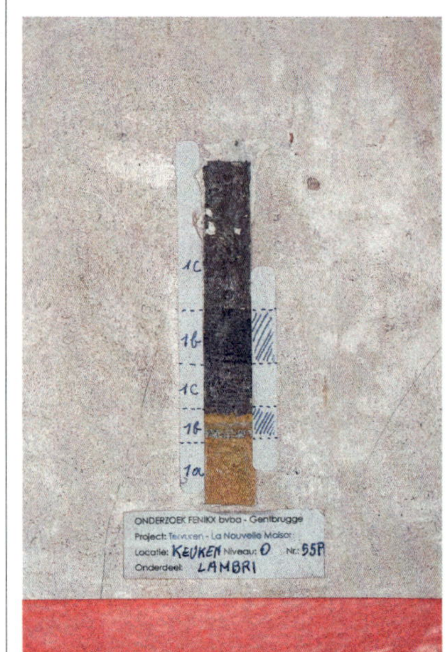

A stratigraphic window at the level of the black frieze in the kitchen, revealing the surprising colours (deep yellow and dark grey).

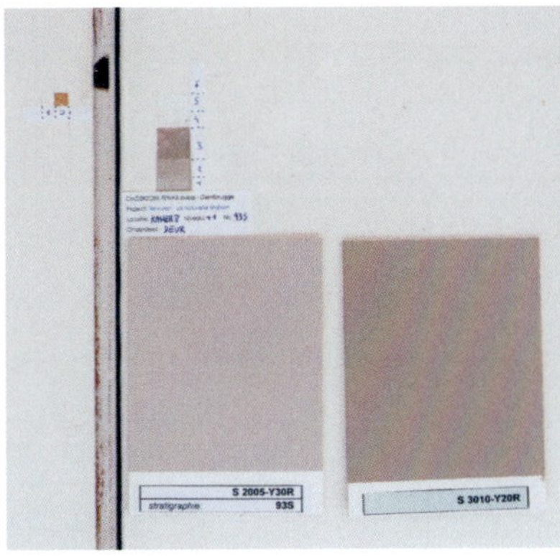

A stratigraphic window on an interior door, along with the colour samples that were applied to assess the consequences of the colour scheme in its context and to make the final decisions.

All of the colours of the painted finishes.

A stratigraphic window on the inside of the basement windows, revealing that they were finished with an oil-based paint containing light metallic particles.

The dismantling of the later kitchen fittings provided an insight into the successive states and finishes, particularly the granite bases and skirting boards. The findings confirmed and added depth to what François Hers (see 3.3) remembered of the original kitchen.

The original wooden floor of the first storey had undergone modifications for electrical work and was therefore covered with a new wooden floor. The green boards in the photo confirm the previous existence of a built-in cupboard, as depicted in the original plans. Due to the added flooring, the interior doors had been shortened, and the skirting boards had been raised. During the restoration, the original floor was restored, the interior doors were extended, and the skirting boards were repositioned to the correct height.

To restore the hygrothermal behaviour of the house, later unsuitable paint layers were completely stripped down to the original lime plaster. This is unusual, as it erases traces of historical evolution. However, one advantage was that marks of alterations and repairs became visible, allowing this information to be cross-referenced with the building history research.

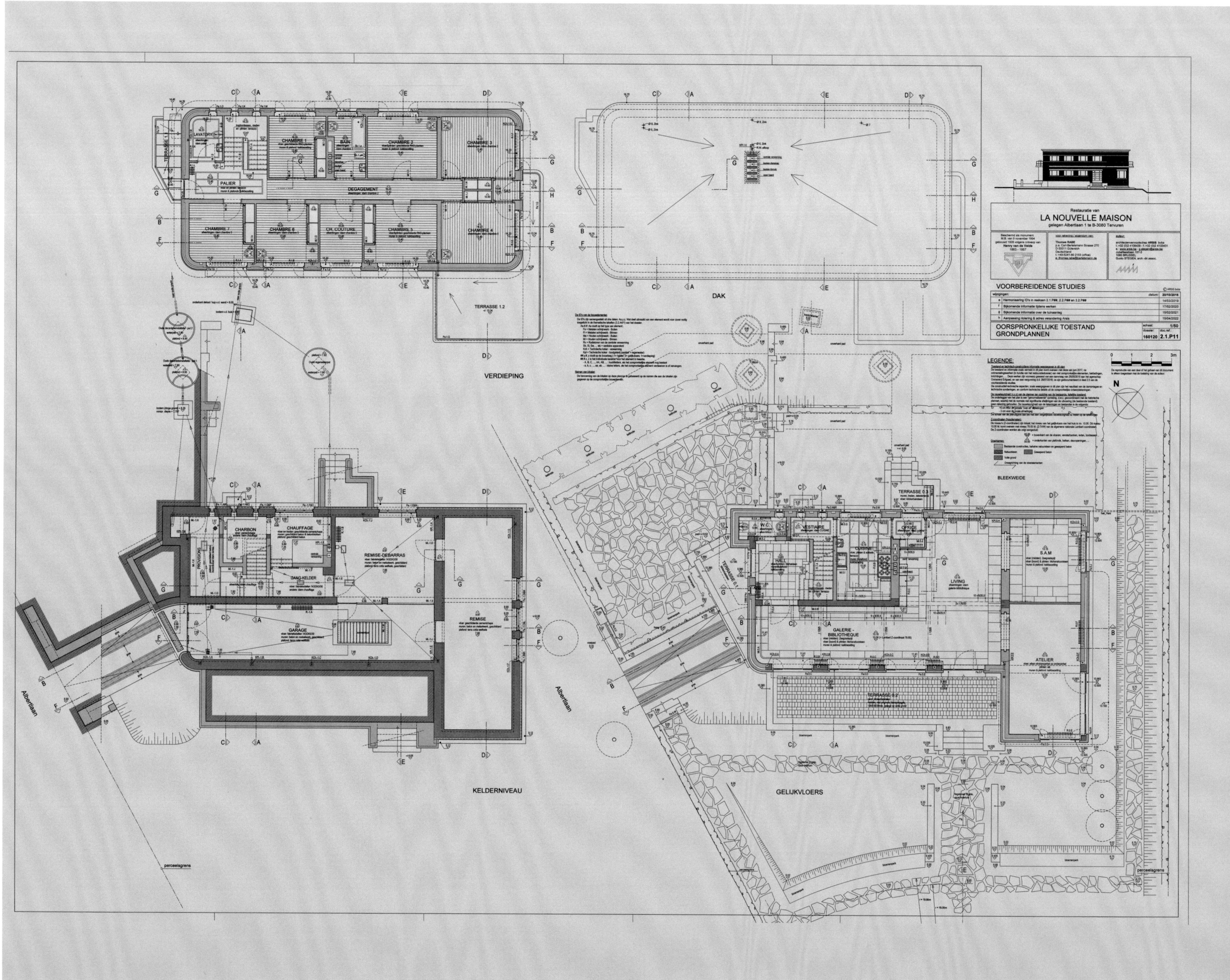
Restauratie van
LA NOUVELLE MAISON
gelegen Albertlaan 1 te B-3080 Tervuren
Beschermd als monument
M.B. van 9 november 1994
gebouwd 1928 volgens ontwerp van
Henry van de Velde
1863 - 1957
voor rekening / eigendom van:
Thomas RABE
p.a. Carl-Bertelsmann Strasse 270
D-33311 Gütersloh
Deutschland
t.:+49-5241-80 2153 (office)
e.:thomas.rabe@bertelsmann.de
auteur:
architectenvennootschap ARSIS bvba
t.:+32 (0)2 4108439 - f.:+32 (0)2 4103431
e.: www.arsis.be - g.stegen@arsis.be
Jubelfeestlaan 157-3
1080 BRUSSEL
Guido STEGEN, arch.-dir.assoc.
VOORBEREIDENDE STUDIES
© ARSIS bvba
wijzigingen: datum: 20/10/2016
e Harmonisering ID's in reeksen 2.1.P##, 2.2.P## en 3.2.P## 14/03/2019
f Bijkomende informatie tijdens werken 17/02/2020
g Bijkomende informatie over de tuinaanleg 15/02/2021
h Aanpassing riolering & adres verandering Arsis 15/04/2022
OORSPRONKELIJKE TOESTAND
GRONDPLANNEN
schaal: 1/50
dossier: 160120
doc.ref.: 2.1.P11
LEGENDE:
0 1 2 3m
De reproductie van een deel of het geheel van dit document is alleen toegestaan met de toelating van de auteur.
N
VERDIEPING
DAK
KELDERNIVEAU
GELIJKVLOERS
LAVATORY
CHAMBRE 1
BAIN
CHAMBRE 2
CHAMBRE 3
PALIER
DEGAGEMENT
CHAMBRE 7
CHAMBRE 6
CH. COUTURE
CHAMBRE 5
CHAMBRE 4
TERRASSE 1.2
CHARBON
CHAUFFAGE
REMISE-DEBARRAS
PROVISIONS
GANG-KELDER
GARAGE
REMISE
VESTIAIRE
OFFICE
CUISINE
HALL
LIVING
S.A.M
GALERIE - BIBLIOTHEQUE
ATELIER
TERRASSE 0.2
TERRASSE 0.3
TERRASSE 0.1
BLEEKWEIDE
Albertlaan
perceelsgrens

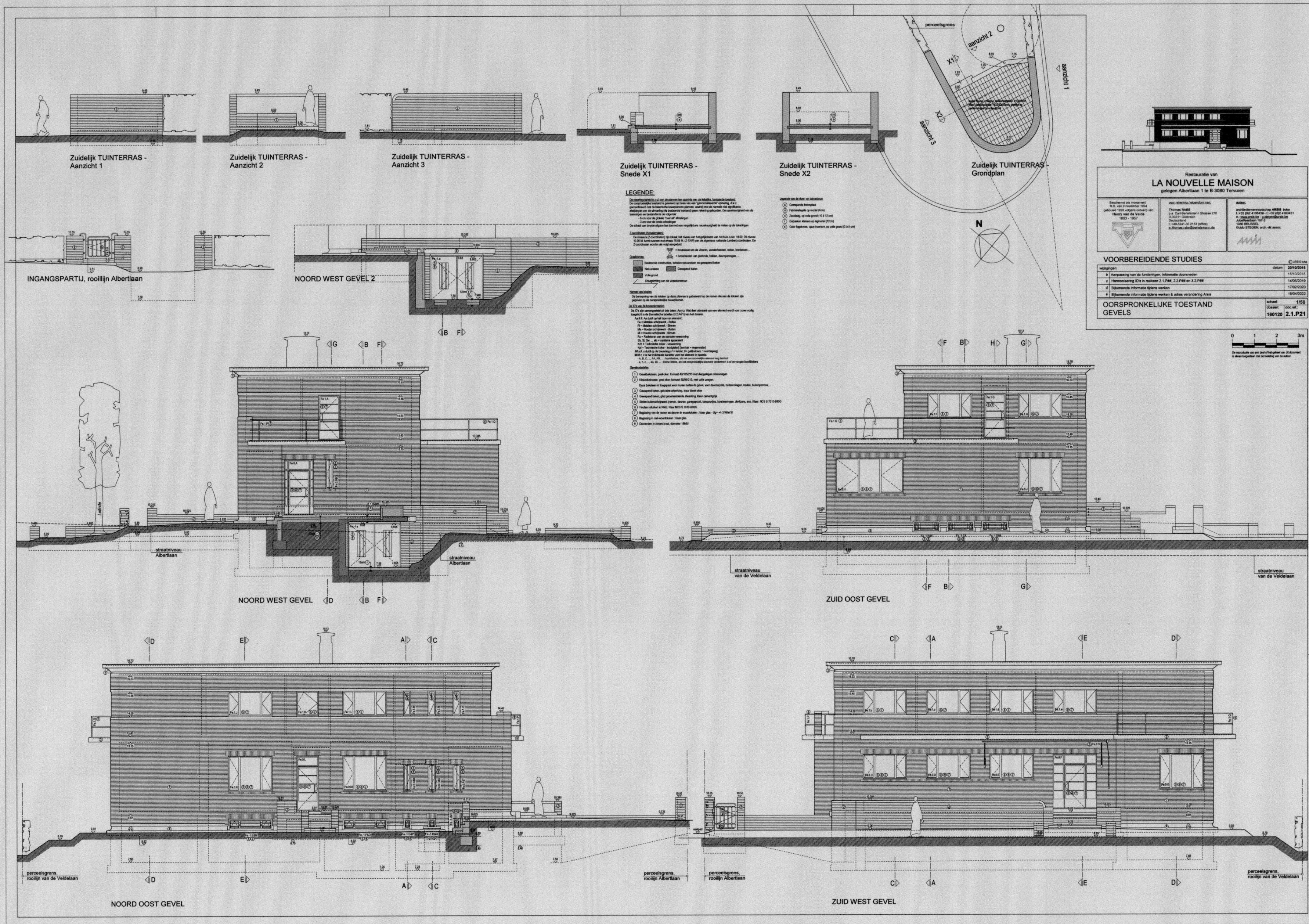

Zuidelijk TUINTERRAS - Aanzicht 1
Zuidelijk TUINTERRAS - Aanzicht 2
Zuidelijk TUINTERRAS - Aanzicht 3
Zuidelijk TUINTERRAS - Snede X1
Zuidelijk TUINTERRAS - Snede X2
Zuidelijk TUINTERRAS - Grondplan
perceelsgrens
aanzicht 1
aanzicht 2
aanzicht 3
N
LEGENDE:
INGANGSPARTIJ, rooilijn Albertlaan
NOORD WEST GEVEL 2
NOORD WEST GEVEL
ZUID OOST GEVEL
NOORD OOST GEVEL
ZUID WEST GEVEL
straatniveau Albertlaan
straatniveau van de Veldelaan
perceelsgrens, rooilijn van de Veldelaan
perceelsgrens, rooilijn Albertlaan
Restauratie van
LA NOUVELLE MAISON
gelegen Albertlaan 1 te B-3080 Tervuren
Beschermd als monument
M.B. van 9 november 1994
gebouwd 1928 volgens ontwerp van
Henry van de Velde
1863 - 1957
voor rekening / eigendom van:
Thomas RABE
p.a. Carl-Bertelsmann Strasse 270
D-33311 Gütersloh
Deutschland
t.:+49-5241-80 2153 (office)
e.:thomas.rabe@bertelsmann.de
auteur:
architectenvennootschap ARSIS bvba
t.:+32 (0)2 4108439 - f.:+32 (0)2 4103431
e.: www.arsis.be - g.stegen@arsis.be
Jubelfeestlaan 157-3
1080 BRUSSEL
Guido STEGEN, arch.-dir.assoc.
VOORBEREIDENDE STUDIES
© ARSIS bvba
wijzigingen: datum: 20/10/2016
b Aanpassing van de funderingen, informatie doorsneden 15/10/2018
c Harmonisering ID's in reeksen 2.1.P##, 2.2.P## en 3.2.P## 14/03/2019
d Bijkomende informatie tijdens werken 17/02/2020
e Bijkomende informatie tijdens werken & adres verandering Arsis 15/04/2022
OORSPRONKELIJKE TOESTAND
GEVELS
schaal: 1/50
dossier: 160120
doc.ref.: 2.1.P21
0 1 2 3m
De reproductie van een deel of het geheel van dit document is alleen toegestaan met de toelating van de auteur.

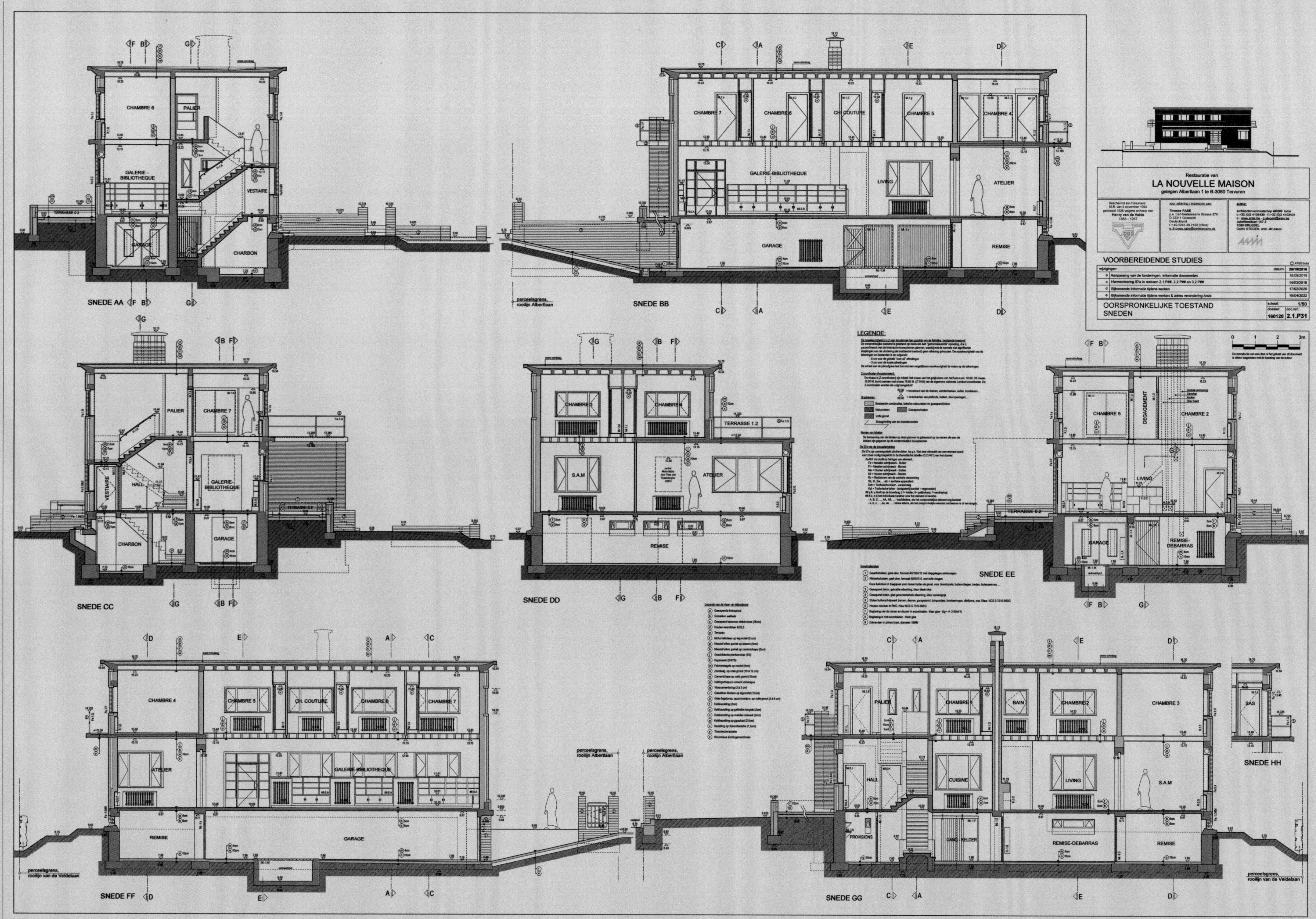

SNEDE AA
SNEDE BB
SNEDE CC
SNEDE DD
SNEDE EE
SNEDE FF
SNEDE GG
SNEDE HH
CHAMBRE 6
PALIER
GALERIE-BIBLIOTHEQUE
VESTIAIRE
GARAGE
CHARBON
CHAMBRE 7
CHAMBRE 6
CH. COUTURE
CHAMBRE 5
CHAMBRE 4
LIVING
ATELIER
REMISE
HALL
TERRASSE 1.2
TERRASSE 0.2
S.A.M
CHAMBRE 3
CHAMBRE 2
DEGAGEMENT
REMISE-DEBARRAS
CUISINE
BAIN
SAS
PROVISIONS
GANG - KELDER
perceelsgrens, rooilijn Albertlaan
perceelsgrens, rooilijn van de Veldelaan
LEGENDE:
Restauratie van
LA NOUVELLE MAISON
gelegen Albertlaan 1 te B-3080 Tervuren
VOORBEREIDENDE STUDIES
OORSPRONKELIJKE TOESTAND
SNEDEN
1/50
160120
2.1.P31

Comfort Analysis and Energy Audit

The actual measured heating consumption in the last three years before the purchase of La Nouvelle Maison varied between 80 and 128 kWh/m²/year, with an average 104kWh/m²/year.[45] According to the energy performance certificate (EPC) prepared at the time of sale, the calculated energy score was 760kWh/m²/year,[46] which represents 730% of the actual measured consumption in EPC.[47] The low actual consumption highlights the priority of identifying and addressing sources of discomfort, as further insulation would yield negligible energy savings. In fact, the payback time for the energy and carbon invested in additional insulation would exceed 100 years. In contrast, reducing discomfort (such as cold radiance and draughts) and addressing structural issues (such as cold bridges and condensation damage) can significantly enhance energy savings. Mitigating discomfort allows for a comparable level of comfort at lower air temperatures, resulting in energy savings. During the preparations for the restoration (from early 2016 to late 2018), the house was heated in a controlled manner to a constant temperature of 18°C. During this period, heating consumption fluctuated between 101 and 123 kWh/m²/year, or an average of 112 kWh/m²/year. Over these 18 months, measurements were also taken of temperature, humidity, comfort temperature, and energy consumption.

Thermography and Airtightness

Thermography is a form of energy imaging that reveals temperature differences in walls, floors, and ceilings. These differences may indicate air leaks or areas where insulation is inadequate, potentially leading to energy loss and discomfort. The airtightness of the external envelope is assessed through both overpressure and underpressure testing. Initially, the heated volume is overpressurised, allowing thermographic images of the building envelope's exterior to display the escaping warm air. To better understand the path of this airflow, smoke is released indoors at suspected leak sites, allowing observers to see where it escapes on the outside. Afterwards, the heated volume is depressurised, and thermographic images are taken on the inside of the external envelope in the same manner.

Such investigations provide information on the airtightness of the exterior envelope (v50) and the ventilation ratio (n50). According to energy standards, houses like La Nouvelle Maison, which do not have controlled mechanical ventilation, are allowed to lose a maximum of three times their volume per hour (n50 < 3). Prior to the restoration, the measured value of n50 was 3.91—almost good enough! That is, according to the standard, because there is no simple correlation between energy consumption and airtightness.

These values apply to the house as a whole; it is a global quantitative approach. In contrast, airtightness measurement combined with thermography is a qualitative method. It provides information on specific issues that need addressing, such as the precise locations of major air or thermal leaks and cold surfaces. For instance, the study revealed significant outside airflows in the wooden floors of the first storey and in the cavities of the roof's T-rib slabs. These cavities connected with openings in the façades, cooling the floors and ceilings. During the restoration, the identified sources of discomfort and air loss were resolved through targeted local interventions.

Targeted intervention is only possible after thorough investigation and after situating local deficiencies within an overall energy and comfort objective – no blanket interventions without significant improvements in comfort and energy efficiency.

Survey of the Garden's Sanitary and Historical Condition

The survey and mapping of the garden, including the topography, brick structures, underground pipes and sewers, and plantings, laid the groundwork for further investigations related to the garden.

The plantings were dated, and their health was assessed to determine their life expectancy and potential future role in the restored garden. The evolution of the topography was established through examination of the surface and subsurface levels, alongside comparisons with historical iconography. The objective was to restore the topography to its original state.

All underground pipes, connections, and equipment of the sewerage system were mapped using cameras and smoke. It was discovered that they had undergone several extensive modifications over time, resulting in chaotic underground water drainage. The project planned for a complete renovation of the external sewerage system to comply with new wastewater

[45] For this figure, only the net heated living area is considered, which is 256 m²; the unheated basement level is not included.

[46] The Energy Performance Certificate (EPC) states 507 kWh/m²/year, but it considers an area of 384 m², i.e., including the basement level. For comparison with the actual consumption, based on the actual heated area: 507 * 384/256 = 760 kWh/m²/year.

[47] It is widely acknowledged that discrepancies between the EPC calculation and actual performance can be substantial. On average, the calculated value in the EPC is four times higher than the real figure. Moreover, the older the house, the greater the difference tends to be.

Thermography before the restoration. When the house is pressurised, warm air escapes, revealing air leaks (such as where the façade brickwork meets the concrete cornice) and less-insulated parts of the building envelope (such as ducts containing heating pipes or radiator niches), made visible by warm colours.

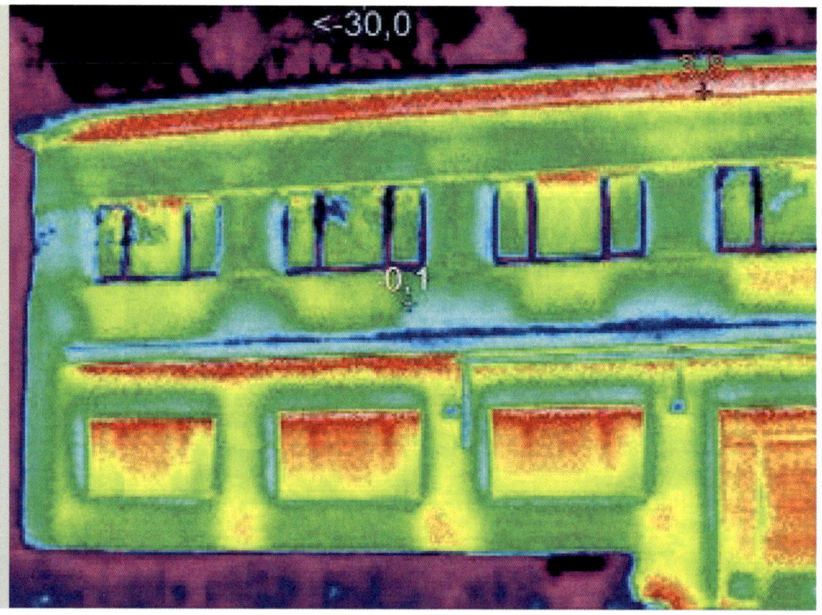

To better understand the path of leaking air, smoke is dispersed inside at the suspected starting point of the leak, and the exterior is observed to see where the smoke escapes from. Here, leaks at the cornice and near the wooden floor of the first floor are clearly visible.

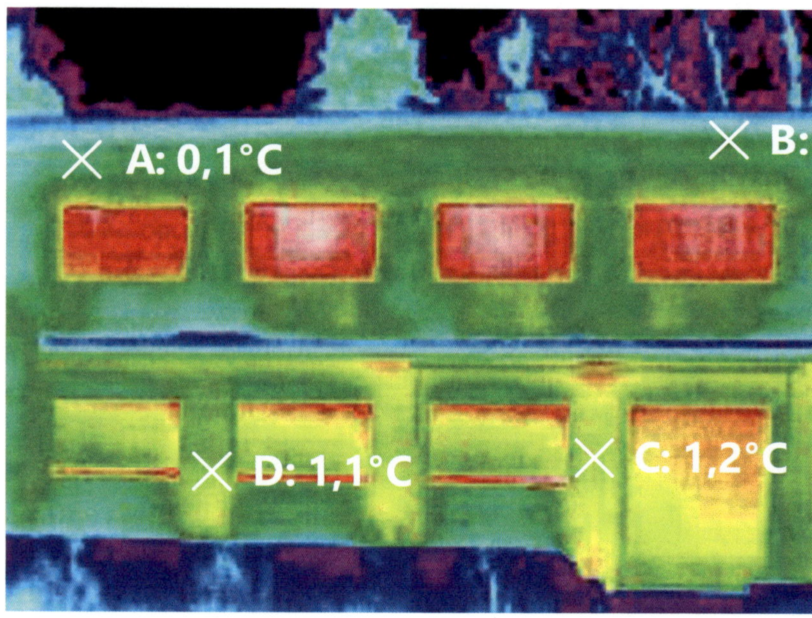

Thermography after the restoration: the weak points, such as the air leak beneath the cornice, are no longer present.

With negative pressure in the house, cold air enters, and the air leaks are visible in cold colours, in this case where cold air can penetrate the wooden floor joists of the first-storey structure and subsequently enter through gaps in the skirting boards.

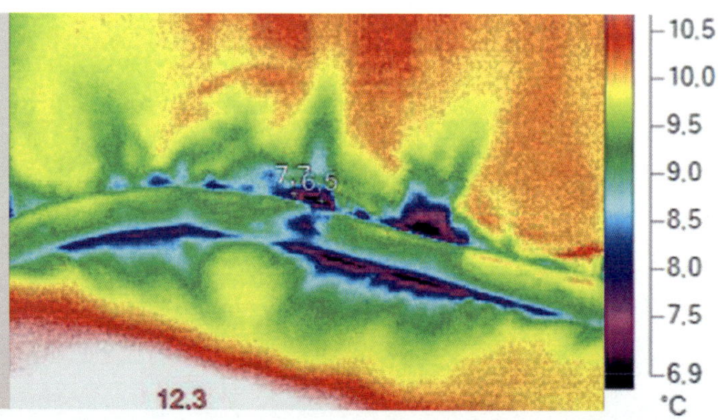

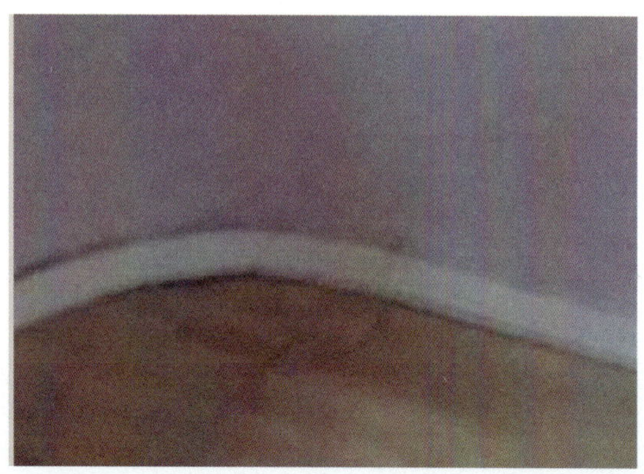

[48] Death of Henry van de Velde.

[49] Koninklijke Bibliotheek AML, FSX470, Nelly Hers: Letter to Van de Velde, Brussels, 29 February 1956.

[50] Ruskin, 'The Lamp of Memory', 1849.

regulations. The section of the sewerage system in glazed stoneware beneath the building was found to be original and still in good condition, and it was retained in its original state.

A SPECIAL WITNESS

After Henry van de Velde left Tervuren for Oberägeri in 1947, La Nouvelle Maison was leased to the family of Joseph and Nelly Hers and their three children, François, Elisabeth, and Myriam. Joseph had previously served as the secretary-general of the Belgian-funded railways in China (1905–37). The Hers family was art-loving, diplomatically engaged, and deeply affectionate towards the house. Van de Velde had rented it out furnished, complete with artworks, a piano, the library, a book archive in the basement, and a garden that was still actively maintained. This arrangement proved beneficial for both van de Velde and the Hers family, who had just returned from China and possessed few furnishings of their own.

The Hers family in 1952 in the garden of La Nouvelle Maison.

From 1947 to 1957,[48] van de Velde in Switzerland and the Hers family in Tervuren corresponded frequently, primarily discussing technical matters, maintenance, and other related issues. This correspondence serves as a valuable resource for the restoration, revealing van de Velde's priorities, his proposed solutions, and the challenges he encountered. Additionally, the letters convey the joy and beauty that the house brought to the Hers family. In 1956, Nelly Hers wrote to van de Velde:

> Dear Sir,
> You know how much I cherish your house;
> I consider it my lucky charm.
> I have always felt completely happy in this
> little paradise, and I cannot imagine
> ever having to leave it. I will forever be
> grateful for the joy you have brought us through
> its light and beauty![49]

François Hers, the son, lived in La Nouvelle Maison from 1947 to 1964, occupying the house in the furnished state that van de Velde had left it. He proved to be an invaluable source of information for the restoration, both regarding the house and its furnishings, as well as the garden. The influence of the house, with its artistic contents and library, was, as he believes, significant in shaping him as a person, artist and founder of Le Protocol de Nouveaux Commanditaires.

MINOR ORGANISATIONAL REQUIREMENTS FOR GOOD RESTORATION

The success of a restoration hinges, to a minor extent, on a prior assessment of the envisaged end result. Preserving and restoring the cohesion of the whole begins with meticulous and systematic attention to the specific materials involved – which can be termed piecemeal engineering. However, this process is sometimes compromised by enthusiasm and haste. Conversely, an overly slow approach and strict adherence to methodology can also prove frustrating. There is a natural tendency for thought to outpace the careful listening to what things want to be, which can jeopardise the integrity of the monument. This resonates with Ruskin's sentiment regarding restoration: 'it means the most total destruction which a building can suffer'.[50]

There are small, practical methods to maintain a 'conscious and systematic' approach, helping to mitigate the risk of 'total destruction' and playing a crucial role in the outcome. These methods need to function in harmony; individually, they lose their significance for the success that can arise from their collective implementation.

Identification

Restoration, with precision and perfection, largely hinges on procedure and control: identifying where, what, and how. To provide the 'where' with sufficient local context, both in intention and outcome, each component of the building is assigned a unique ID. These identifiers are crafted to be as clear as possible to prevent potential errors. The IDs consist of three parts. The first part relates to the specifications corresponding to the building trade. For example, 'Me' denotes exterior wood joinery; 'Sw' refers to sanitary fittings; and 'Fi' indicates interior forgings. The second part indicates the building level (-1, 0, 1). The third part represents the order on that level, moving in a counterclockwise direction. Capital letters signify that the element is original, while lowercase letters indicate that the original element has been lost or replaced. Numbers denote elements that did not originally exist.

For those involved in the implementation there is no need to refer to a detailed list to know most of the essential information about each element. This helps to prevent significant mistakes. Additionally, components of larger elements are also labelled, with the initial code reflecting the ID of the main part to which they belong.

Safe Shed

Disassembly is akin to 'the bull in a china shop' when it comes to restoration. Avoiding disassembly can prevent a great deal of distress; however, there are times when it is necessary for practical and quality reasons. In principle, removed or disassembled parts should remain on-site unless the restoration architect or main contractor provides explicit approval for their removal. Work meetings should not take place in external workshops, as this removes the context necessary for informed decision-making and can lead to speculation. The safe shed serves as a storage area with restricted access, where disassembled parts are organised and kept safe. It houses both restored and non-restored components, and a regular inventory and report of its contents are maintained.

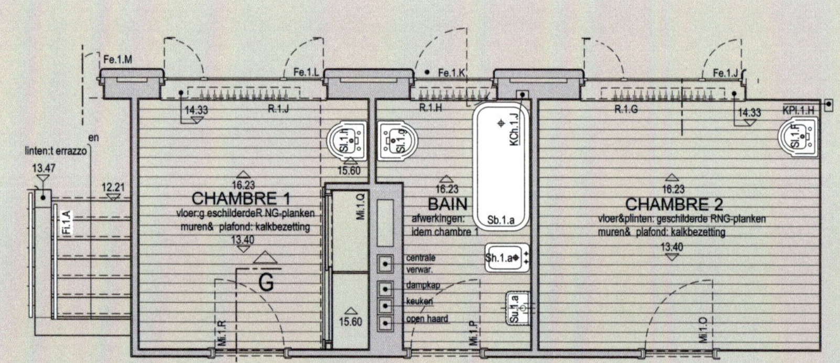

The plans include the unique IDs referenced in the descriptions of the works.

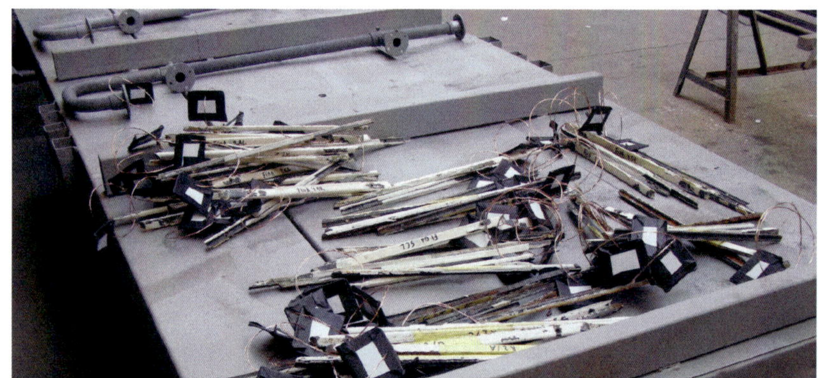

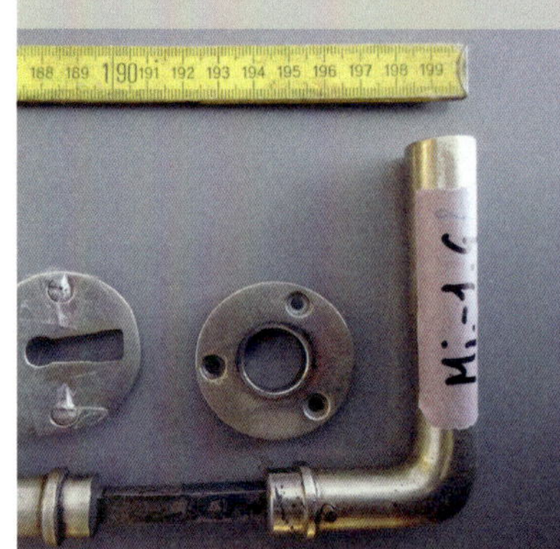

All elements, or parts of elements, were permanently labelled with their unique ID both before, during, and after their restoration – as were the reconstructed new parts.

The contents of the safe storage area are constantly changing, as is the organisation of the items.

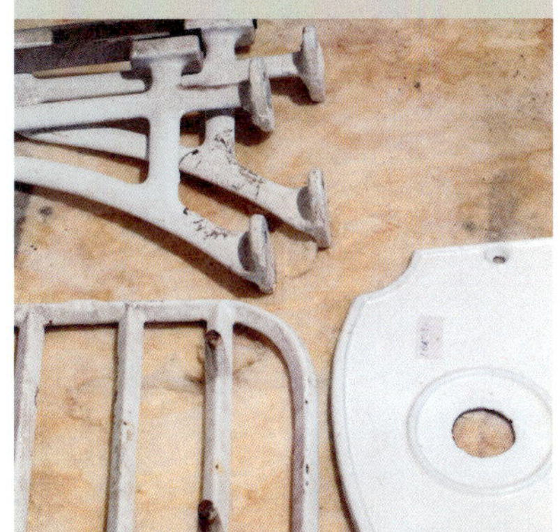

Sanitary fixtures had been relocated in part due to past modifications; some had been removed but were fortunately stored in the basement. This made it possible to restore them to their original locations after renovations. This exemplifies a philosophy of circularity and 'using what you have' in action. Careful preparation is required to identify wandering materials and valuable components.

Following past construction work and the need to preserve raw materials, original bricks, flagstones, and terrace tiles had become scattered and overgrown across the property, with some left in stacks. During the garden restoration, they were found, collected, and optimally reused as part of the restoration process.

The basement space, which served as a safe storage area during the restoration work, has been repurposed as a room for the conservation of historical materials and for the study of the restoration archive.

The conservation of historical materials includes original components that were not reused in the restoration, materials on which tests were conducted, and samples.

Workplace 'on Site'

The safe shed is not to be used as a workshop; a designated on-site workshop is available for that purpose. This workshop is equipped for minor repairs, and most construction workers carry basic tools for such tasks in their site vehicles.

Unfortunately, it is often observed that the more global the logistics and the larger the machinery, the greater the potential for 'total destruction' (Ruskin). Consequently, local and on-site repairs demand a high level of skill from specialised craftspeople. Manual precision work remains essential. There is a prevalent myth that global logistics and larger machines enhance results: 'Let us not deceive ourselves in this important matter!' (Ruskin)

In the on-site workshop, interventions are discussed, concrete agreements are established, and tests are conducted. It is a setting that requires all parties to concentrate and adhere to the specific scope of the problem. This sense of 'domesticity' renders the discussions more concrete than abstract, effectively curbing speculation.

... Don't Lose Your Bearings ...

Once again, the aim is to 'give the benefit of the doubt' to what exists. If things have endured for decades or even centuries, they likely functioned well. In this context, 'bearings' refer not only to the components themselves but also to their location, orientation, and other details. This encompasses everything from small elements, such as a screw, its thread, and screw hole, to larger components, like a glass pane and its proper position or a lock fitted into the correct door. Disassembly demands meticulous orderliness, including marking, positioning, and labelling down to the smallest part. This example may seem trivial, but losing a screw and replacing it with something only vaguely similar can severely hinder proper functioning. Manually screwing screws and nuts in and out helps to avoid damaging the 'bearings.' While machines may seem like a time-saving solution, they often end up damaging the threads and heads of screws and nuts, which are crucial for ensuring that everything aligns correctly during assembly. For instance, steel joinery used to operate with tolerances of 0.1 mm, while wood joinery worked with tolerances of 1 mm. In this context, precise benchmarks are vital for delivering quality efficiently and cost-effectively. The introduction of sealing joints in windows has diminished the need for such precision, fostering the misconception that these older, precise components can still function effectively within today's larger tolerances for sealed windows. Once again: 'do not let us deceive ourselves!'.

For heritage buildings, there is a significant difference between a weld, a rivet, and a bolt; while they serve similar purposes, each tells a different story about construction, maintenance, and repair. For instance, there has been a tacit intergenerational agreement among joiners that round-headed screws are important to prevent damage when disassembling or accessing components for maintenance. This shared knowledge is an essential aspect of heritage, supporting sustainable use and conservation. Glue, nails, countersunk screws, and round-headed screws are not merely interchangeable; each has its specific role and significance.

The workplace on site was set up in the garage, adjacent to the safe storage area and meeting room. This sense of 'domesticity' facilitates decisions about specific local issues, supporting an effective restoration strategy.

Not only the shape of the screw, nut, bolt, its seating, thread, and chamfer of the screw head, etc., matters; the material was also chosen according to the 'law of help', ensuring maximum longevity of the most critical parts. This concept involves deliberately choosing which component will sacrifice itself for the preservation of the whole to limit the scope of any potential repairs. Conservation also means preserving this way of thinking and sustainable design.

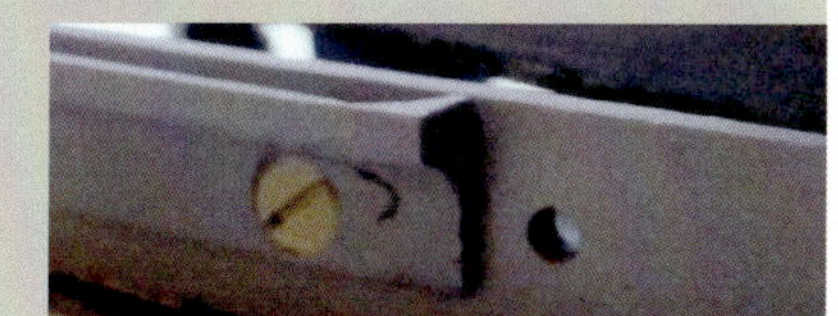

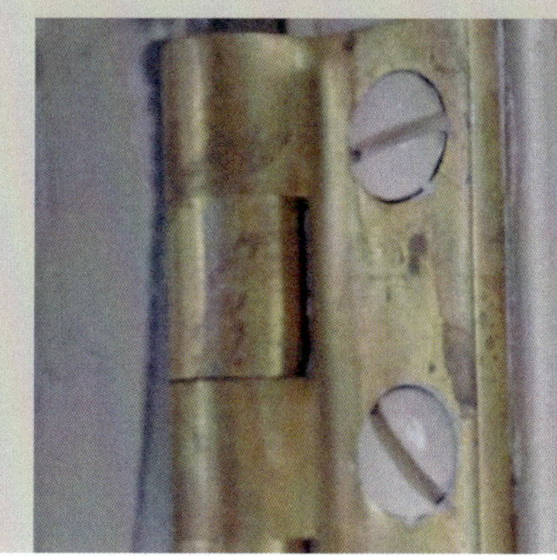

'The right piece in the right place' is an adage that already applied during the construction of La Nouvelle Maison in 1928, if only because of the high precision required for the proper functioning of doors, windows, radiators, taps, etc. Many pieces were numbered – not just fittings, as shown in this photo. Even the bricks were marked with around five different codes, depending on the specific shape and the sides that were sanded.

Sometimes things go wrong, and 'one loses one's bearings'. Labels are not replaced, as seen here with the hinges of the interior doors and the glass retainers of the windows; old, forged hinges have tapered edges, so that they fit tightly into their precisely-chiselled wooden recesses, securely supporting the door; glass retainers are not interchangeable, as the screw holes and bores can differ by mere tenths of a millimetre. This can result in damage to the screws or the need to re-drill the holes, which nowadays can no longer be done with the same precision as before.

Handling original components carefully and systemically to avoid damage is much simpler and faster. Such components are often no longer available for purchase, or the alternatives are far less robust. Making replicas is expensive, time-consuming, and they are never perfectly identical, resulting in poor functionality.

The Example of Concrete

La Nouvelle Maison dates from the initial heyday of reinforced concrete,[51] featuring both prefabricated and on-site cast elements.

The largest volume of concrete is unreinforced and was used to cast the entire basement, as well as the thick central wall of the ground floor in situ. This type of concrete is particularly noteworthy; it is a living material known as concrete K,[52] a disintegrated mix that is non-capillary and unreinforced, boasting a very high moisture buffering capacity. In some areas, such as the beam supports, it has been replaced by a carbonation-resistant mix for reinforced concrete. The groundwater table on the site is often very high, reaching just 50 cm below the lowest floor of the basement. There is no sealing; the floor tiles are laid directly on a sand layer atop the loam soil. Today, it is generally assumed that concrete basements, if they are waterproof at all, typically experience condensation problems, making them unsuitable for storing valuables. However, the basement of La Nouvelle Maison exhibits neither capillary moisture issues nor condensation problems. This can be attributed in part to the clay terraces surrounding the house, which effectively divert precipitation away from the house.

This vast unreinforced, porous yet non-capillary concrete mass also functions as a hygrothermal flywheel, akin to the capabilities of loam structures, acting as a buffer against both cold and heat when necessary. This exemplifies bioclimatics and robustness at its finest, thanks to a consistent application of material expertise. Today, a basement in such conditions would be designed quite differently. Nevertheless, during the restoration process, the decision was made to meticulously preserve the old robust and self-regulating mechanisms, including the restoration of the surrounding topography. Everything works in harmony – this is the 'law of help'.

In terms of reinforced concrete, only the terrace edges, particularly the cornice, were in concerning condition. These areas had been finished with a special architectural top layer on a grey concrete core, which is typically where the reinforcements are contained. This scratch layer consists of a decorative concrete made from a unique mix; it is stripped before the concrete fully hardens. The surface layer is then scraped away, revealing a rough texture with the specially selected aggregates exposed. Restoring a scratch coat with large aggregates can be challenging, especially if the concrete cover is thin (5 to 10 mm). In the restoration process, a choice must be made between repairing with excessive thickness, using a different aggregate, or employing synthetic mortars. A grade with smaller aggregates was chosen in this case. This approach respects the original geometry (avoiding excessive thickness), ensures that the issue is not merely shifted, and helps prevent symptoms of rejection (utilising a purely mineral and hydraulic mortar rather than a synthetic one). For minor repairs, the repair mortars are mixed on-site as prescribed, and in small quantities to accommodate the limited scale of the repairs. Workability and a low water-to-cement ratio are key criteria for formulating an effective compound. Additionally, how the repairs age and respond to moisture is crucial. Colour and granulometry, to the extent that they cannot be reconciled with these considerations, are secondary and do not significantly impact the overall appearance in the case of small repairs.

One could have anticipated that the cornice would pose the most significant challenges. Its angled shape necessitated the use of a fairly stiff concrete mortar, which also featured a low water-to-cement ratio for enhanced carbonation resistance, as was standard practice at the time. Such a concrete mortar is difficult to compact, making it challenging to avoid air inclusions. Consequently, cavities often remain in the concrete, particularly at the bottom and in corners, where reinforcement meets formwork. If the reinforcements within these cavities are subsequently exposed to water, rust will inevitably begin to develop. This was indeed the case; however, it turned out to be fortunate, as it allowed for localised repairs of the deficiencies. The damage was limited and contained, attributable to the superior quality of the concrete, which significantly exceeded current standards. The concrete had not yet carbonated and remained fully capable of

[51] Between 1920 and 1930, the annual concrete production for buildings in Belgium increased from 0.5 million tons to 4.5 million tons, reaching 6 million tons by 1939, before dropping again to 0.5 million tons during World War II. Source: TVn144, WTCB-BBRI, 1982, fig. 1.

[52] Type K concrete is a cement-lime concrete, still referenced in the now-discontinued Type Specification 104 of the Buildings Administration of the Belgian Ministry of Public Works. Reference 26.0/4-9°, 1963 edition (ref.104/63/0).

[53] Corrosion is an electrochemical process. When applying cathodic protection, the corrosion potential of the metal to be protected is reduced, thereby decreasing the (rate of) corrosion. The reduction of the corrosion potential can be achieved through impressed direct current or through galvanic current that is generated between two metals with different corrosion potentials. Sacrificial anodes for concrete conservation are typically made of zinc, which sacrifices itself to protect the reinforcing steel.

protecting the reinforcements. Additionally, the now-obsolete softer reinforcing steel, which has a low carbon content, will corrode less expansively, further mitigating potential issues.

Local minor repairs to reinforced concrete are carried out carefully to avoid causing significant further damage, primarily for preventive reasons. In areas prone to persistent water exposure and corrosion risks, such as the eaves and cornice, cathodic protection using sacrificial anodes was added.[53] This contemporary preservation technique for reinforced concrete helps to prevent the need for extensive preventive replacements of additional concrete.

The largest volume of concrete is unreinforced: the special 'concrete K' used for the thick walls in the basement and the central load-bearing wall on the ground floor. Its significant hygrothermal inertia enhances comfort in the living areas and ensures that the basement spaces remain perfectly dry.

The bright, raw, architectural concrete with a scratch coat plays a key role in the refined aesthetics of the façade. The play of light on its mineral surface makes it shine, and, during rainy weather, it blends in with the bricks due to its porous nature.

The colour, texture, detailing, proportions – all this had changed over the years. The edges had been raised, unsuccessful concrete repairs had been carried out, some sections had been coated with waterproofing, the entire surface had been repainted, and the chimney capstone had inevitably eroded due to acidic smoke.

It is still common for concrete to be completely replaced due to the belief that it has been too severely acidified by the carbon dioxide in the air. The photo shows an acidification drill test using phenolphthalein on undamaged sections (which turn red when not acidified), demonstrating that the quality of the concrete there is still 'as new', even better than what can be made today. It is often found that historic concrete, up until the 1960s, is very resistant and only shows local defects. A 'glocal' approach to this means 'restoring'. Local defects are usually gravel nests, which occur when relatively dry concrete is used, as seen at the lower edge of the cornice in the other photo.

Exposed concrete subjected to significant rain impact was given additional protection against reinforcement corrosion through cathodic protection with sacrificial zinc anodes. These anodes spontaneously activate when the conditions for corrosion arise. As long as the steel is embedded in non-acidified concrete, this does not occur.

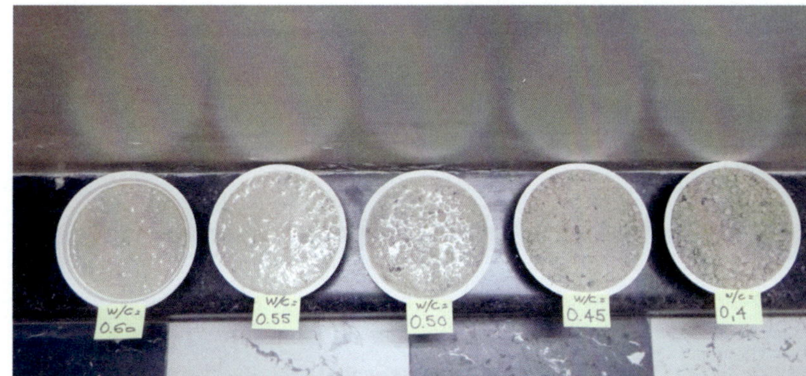

Local repairs within a 'glocal' approach require the right mortar in the right place, with the primary consideration being that it must be 'functional'. Mortar is not meant to sustain itself but to contribute effectively to the preservation of the whole. Repair mortars are therefore artisanally formulated and tested. In the case of small repairs, deviations from the original composition are often necessary to achieve a high-quality result. This leads to visible repairs and a 'humble aesthetic'. The aim should never be to demolish larger sections simply to make repairs invisible. Consistent and small-scale repairs are rarely disruptive.

In the case of the terrace edges, the upper edge had to be recast. For the cornice, it was the drip edge, which had already been replaced with another material and therefore needed to be restituted (recreated) using a mortar compatible with the intact sections. Its upper side was restored to its original, lower level. The chimney capstone was also replaced.

Colour differences between old and new materials can be softened with a silicate-based glaze (ethyl silicate or potassium silicate), as demonstrated in the test between the two tape lines in the photo, reducing the colour difference of the lighter, new drip edge.

The Example of Steel Windows. An Exercise in Modesty

The window and door openings in the façade are fitted with steel windows manufactured by the Brussels-based Van Hamme production company. Many modernist buildings of the period feature windows and doors constructed from these profiles, known as the 'chair profile'. La Nouvelle Maison was included in a publication showcasing the company's reference projects, complete with detail and perspective drawings. To accommodate shutter detailing, the ground-storey steel windows were set into a resin-wood frame that snugly fits into the shell. This wood-resin frame was preserved throughout the restoration, as it was found to be in perfect condition.

On the southwest side on the first storey, the four original three-piece windows had been replaced with aluminium windows. During restoration, these were removed and reconstructed in steel, following the original design.[54] The special fittings, handles, restrictors, condensation trays and other components were recast and reassembled based on the original models. As was the case for all original fittings, they were protected – without the use of artificial patina or varnish – with a microcrystalline wax, allowing a beautiful natural patina to develop over time.

The windows are fitted with single non-insulating glazing. In the case of the small, already burglar-proof windows, the original glass was retained. For the other windows, 6 mm thick laminated glass of a neutral colour was used, without a metal coating, and featuring a subtle 'waviness' that mitigates the harsh reflections commonly associated with contemporary float or mirror glass.[55]

The damage to the windows and doors that needed repair was primarily rust damage, localised at the underside, the bottom rails of the fixed frames, and the beginning of the vertical posts. This damage had occurred, as is often the case, due to a combination of stagnant water and damage to the original protective coating caused by maintenance work, accelerated by – relevantly here – galvanic corrosion of the brass fittings (drip sills, condensation trays).[56] For the restoration, all opening sashes and the central fixed sashes were removed. All fittings, glass, glazing bars, and so on were taken out, and all profiles were sandblasted, locally repaired, metallised, sealed, and repainted.

The restoration of the steel windows sadly exemplifies Ruskin's assertion about 'destruction'. Many of the minor organisational requirements previously mentioned were violated: there was more disassembly than necessary, inadequate labelling, loss of 'bearings', and an overreliance on global logistics that made contextual discussion and control impossible. Perfectly intact protections were unnecessarily sandblasted due to warranty restrictions rather than addressing the transitions between existing and new protections. The complete bare blasting of the steel and renewal of the metallisation promised forty years of rust protection. Yet, as Ruskin warned, 'do not let us deceive ourselves in this important matter': less than a year after completion, rust needed to be mitigated in several areas.

The 'good' news is that, overall, preserving is still better than renewing and replacing. After the restoration, the house underwent another airtightness measurement, revealing that the four new windows performed worse than those that are nearly 100 years old. This issue needed to be resolved post-factum using today's standard solutions: high-maintenance sealing kits. Restoration is, after all, an exercise in modesty.

[54] For the restoration, Forster Retrosteel steel profiles were used, enabling the assembly of the original profile, provided that one of the component profiles was modified.

[55] 'Waviness' refers to an irregular reflection that occurs on a glossy surface when it is not perfectly flat.

[56] Galvanic corrosion occurs in a moist environment when a metal with low corrosion potential (in our case copper and brass), comes into contact with a metal that has a high corrosion potential (in our case steel). This contact leads to aggressive localised corrosion of the metal with the highest corrosion potential.

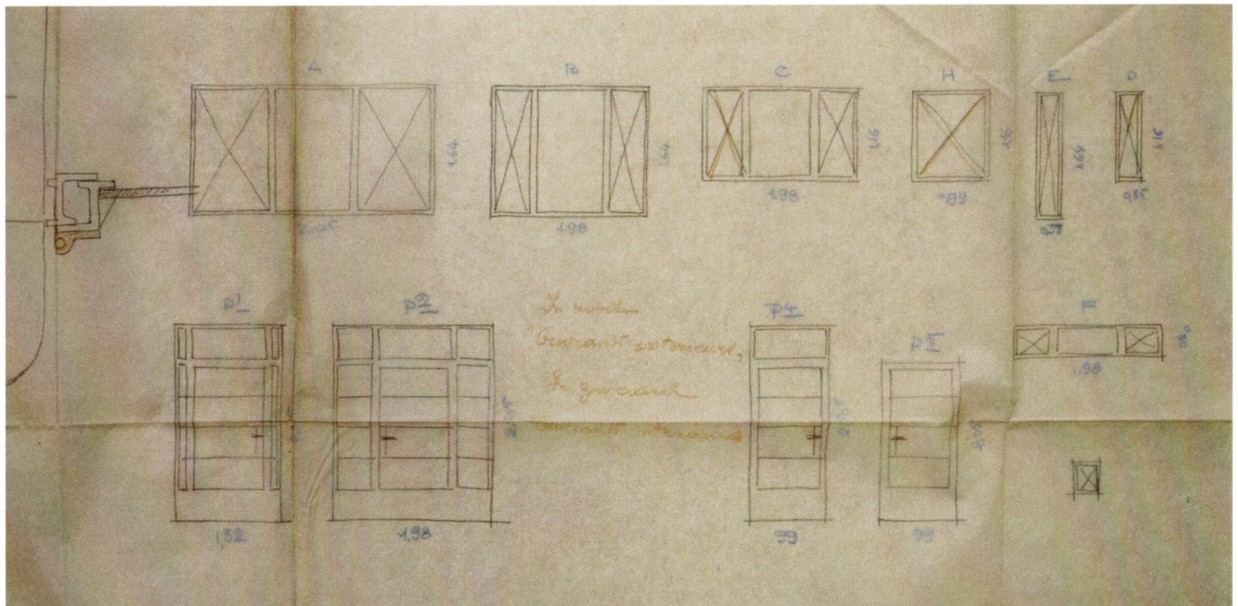

La Cambre, digitised inventory, doc. ID 091/R; date after June 1928. After the selection of the Belvedere façade brick, all width dimensions changed, including the window openings and divisions. All essential information about these changes is committed to paper in this hand-drawn document: sectional details, façade connections, window divisions and opening directions, etc.
This document directly corresponds to the realised construction. For the composition of the window divisions, van de Velde used a constant dimension derived from the width of the bathroom window (99 cm, marked in red on the drawing), which resulted from the new façade design. This is consistently used for all other windows and doors (marked in light red on the drawing), creating a sense of calm and order in the otherwise dynamic and organic façade.

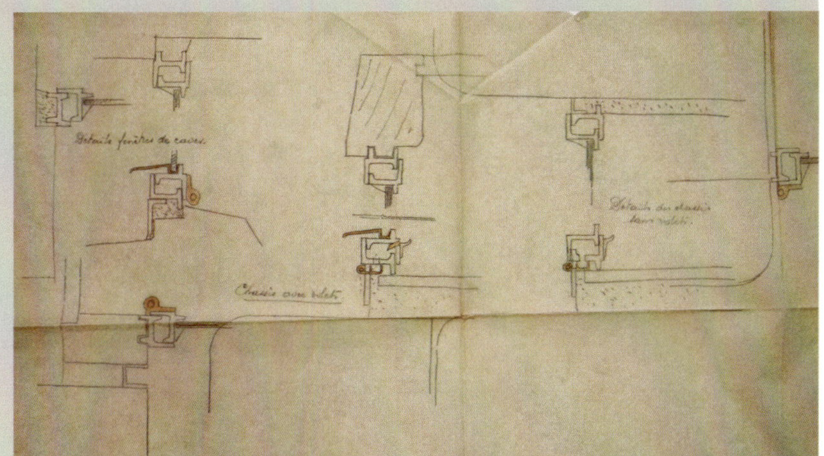

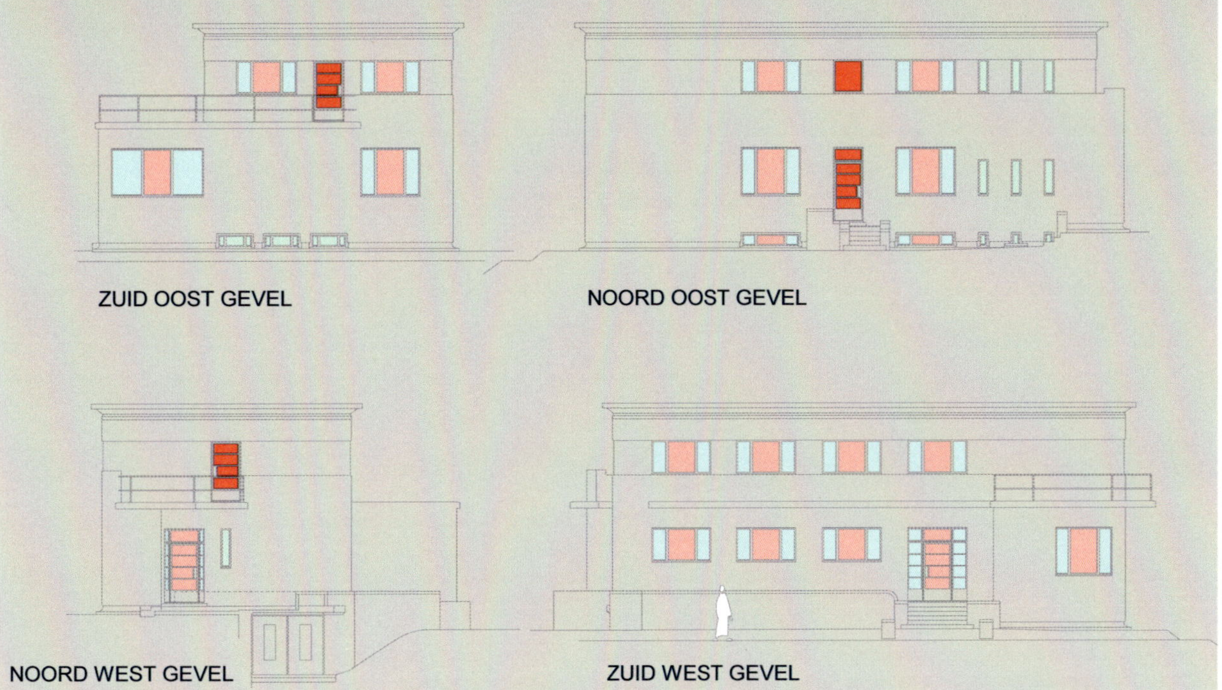

The severe structural damage to the windows and doors was largely found in the lower sections, affecting both fixed and operable sashes. Another common issue was galvanic corrosion, resulting from the combination of a copper alloy and steel. In a humid environment, this combination causes aggressive and highly localised corrosion damage, as seen around the condensation trays, the hinge pots of pivoting windows, and the brass drip edges in cases of water infiltration. Beyond this, there was only very superficial rusting, with little impact on the sections of the steel profiles.

After deconstructing all components to their simplest state and maximising accessible surfaces, the steel parts were stripped of paint using grit blasting. This provided a clear view of the actual damage, and then the 'glocal' routine in consultation was followed for consultation: what repair is necessary? Does the part still function advantageously for everything that is connected with it (Ruskin)? The areas marked in red on the photo are the locations where local repairs were deemed necessary.

In a general renewal of galvanic protection (zinc metallisation), all removable parts were separated, and the glass retainers and glass taken out.

After all local repairs, the frames were metallised (sprayed with molten zinc) and immediately sealed with a sealer. This was finished with a primer and two topcoats based on alkyd resin. The entire finishing layer is only 120 microns thick (max. 150 microns) to ensure that proper functioning is not hindered.

The four windows on the southwest side of the first storey, previously replaced with aluminium frames, were restored to their original design using Forster Retrosteel profiles and matching brass hinges. The brass hardware was recast based on the existing original models.

All brass components of the exterior woodwork were cleaned and finished with a thin layer of microcrystalline wax to achieve a natural bronze-like patina, which will gradually develop organic signs of wear.

For architecture where spatial continuity is fundamental to the experience, the choice of glass is important, particularly its colour, transparency, and reflection. For all windows protected by burglar bars or with very small glass surfaces, the original single glazing was preserved. For the other glazing, a neutral, clear, single-layered glass with a slight wave was chosen.

The wooden shutters on the ground floor led to a unique kind of detailing involving wooden connections between the building shell and steel windows. They serve as a security feature but primarily form an integral part of the exterior envelope, managing heat and cold. Some shutters had been replaced with PVC shutters, which were restored to their original design. These rolling shutters feature an ultra-light and thin profile, without metal hinges, but with natural fibre ribbons interwoven with copper threads for mould protection. There are three types of rollers, chosen for function based on the weight of the shutter, and either built-in or surface-mounted depending on the presence of concrete columns.

The Example of Energy

Many visitors are interested in the heating system of La Nouvelle Maison. The original setup was a central heating system featuring a coal boiler and cast-iron radiators, with water circulation relying on thermosiphon action[57] – nothing extraordinary for its time, except for its exceptionally neat and well-thought-out design.

Over the years, the original boiler was replaced with a gas boiler featuring an atmospheric burner and low water volume. A circulator pump was added, and the open expansion vessel was replaced with a pressure expansion vessel in the basement. These modifications were confined to the components within the heating room. Additionally, hot water production, which initially relied on a gas-fired instantaneous water heater in the bathroom, has since been converted to an electric system.

The restoration has preserved all original elements, with the exception of the manual radiator valves, which were replaced with thermostatic radiator valves based on the original design. The system is designed to function in two distinct ways: it can operate using the original thermosiphon circulation, without a pump, and at a high boiler temperature. Consequently, the new gas boiler was selected for its large water capacity and wide connection diameters. Additionally, the system can be configured to operate with a modern outdoor sensor, circulation pump, and variable heating curves.

The house does not have air conditioning, and therefore lacks cooling for the summer. The bioclimatic processes originally present in the house have been restored, and this appears to be effective. There is exterior sun protection on the ground storey, including awnings and shutters, as well as a series of adiabatic cooling buffers.[58] The large flat roof features a gravel layer that provides similar buffering effects.

Canaries in the Coal Mine

Good houses require minimal attention once the 'law of help' takes effect. Proper maintenance is essential for the ongoing suitability of materials and systems.[59] Residents are also integral to the system we call 'house' – there is interaction, after all. Occupants take care of their homes, just like well-designed houses take care of their residents. A living traditional house provides insights into comfort and health, not through added electronic features, but through the visible responses of its materials. A truly smart house communicates.

For a healthy indoor climate, relative humidity should ideally be maintained between 40% and 65%. As previously mentioned, the large open pores in the walls and finishes help buffer moisture in both directions, stabilising humidity levels. The single glazing in La Nouvelle Maison, along with the curtains, controls the upper limit through condensation, while the natural sisal carpet in the library, seating area, and dining room controls the lower limit.[60] When the air becomes too dry,[61] the carpet loses tension and becomes less tight, providing a visual cue to occupants.

[57] A thermosiphon circulation operates without a circulation pump; instead, water circulates by gravity. The warm water, produced by the boiler, rises, while the cooler water, which has been cooled in the radiators, descends. A sufficient temperature difference and an adequate volume of water are necessary to maintain movement, relying on gravity and requiring no additional energy. Furthermore, well-designed radiators and appropriately sized pipe diameters are essential to minimise pressure losses and maintain consistency. Additionally, the pipes must be sloped, and the radiators should also be slightly tilted.

[58] Adiabatic cooling and heating are bioclimatic mechanisms that utilise energy derived from the phase changes of water. During condensation, heat is released, while cold is produced during evaporation. By harnessing the heat in winter and the cold in summer, fluctuations in indoor temperatures can be limited without the need for additional energy.

[59] Maintenance is the natural continuation of conservation, repair and restoration. Consequently, a maintenance manual for La Nouvelle Maison has been included in the restoration documents. This manual addresses the products, tools, frequencies, and other relevant details.

[60] Originally, there was a sea grass carpet in La Nouvelle Maison, consisting of interwoven carpet tiles measuring 50 × 50 cm. This module defined the boundaries of the Moha limestone at the edges of the living spaces. The van de Veldes were strong advocates for this type of flooring in their homes. Writing from Oberägeri, Henry van de Velde insisted that the worn carpet should not be replaced with another carpet or parquet, although his request was not heeded. During the restoration, it was decided to return to carpeting, not least for the sake of acoustic comfort. Since 50 × 50 cm modules were unavailable and other sizes did not fit within the Moha border, a full sisal carpet was selected. It shares the same colour as the sea grass carpet and is, for the time being, a suitable alternative.

[61] In winter, homes with central radiator heating often become too dry, and La Nouvelle Maison is no exception. When the relative humidity drops below 40%, the sisal carpet begins to expand, leading to the formation of ripples. The carpet is placed on separate padding that is stretched at the edges; at healthy humidity levels, this tension is maintained. The owners wisely opted for primarily natural ventilation through the windows. The kitchen features a natural circulation system that draws air from the basement and expels it through the roof. The wet rooms are equipped with mechanical ventilation that includes a timer, but brief ventilation through the windows is the preferred method. This ventilation strategy, without fans, has the significant advantage in winter of not creating negative pressure in the house. As a result, cold outside air is not drawn in, helping to maintain a less dry and healthier indoor climate.

Window restrictors allow for graduated ventilation, according to the needs of the moment. The curtains not only ensure comfortable lighting levels but also reduce the cold radiating from the glass and increase the glass's ability to condense and keep away excess moisture.

The cast iron radiators were stripped of paint on site, repaired, repainted in their original colour, and fitted with thermostatic valves.

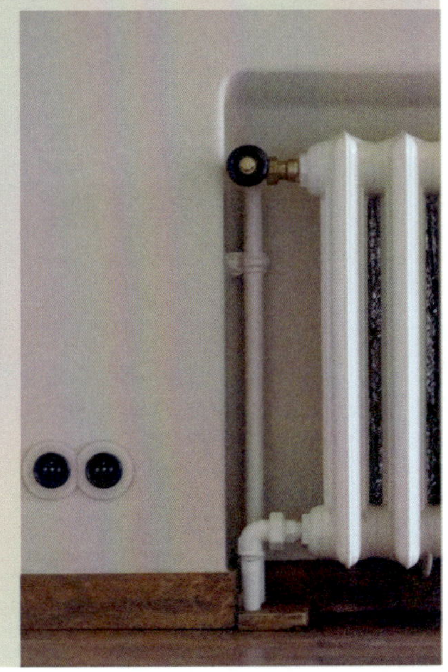

The single glazing causes the excess moisture to condense, recovering energy provided that the condensate is drained away.

The radiator niches, identified as weak points in the building envelope through airtightness measurements and thermography, were insulated with insulating plaster and a heat-reflective foil.

The flat roof was covered with a layer of gravel made from crushed beige limestone. While protecting against thermal shocks, it particularly enhances thermal comfort by condensing and evaporating moisture, significantly increasing thermal inertia, and cooling the roof in the summer (adiabatic cooling).

THE HOUSE'S USE

La Nouvelle Maison continues to function as a residential property, which helps avoid complications associated with some conversions. The spatial distribution of the house remains unchanged, preserving the connections between the rooms on the southwest side. Some doorways that had been closed off at some point were reopened and fitted with replicas of the original doors. Missing details and fittings, or those replaced with inadequate models, were recreated based on historical examples. In the kitchen, custom-made cabinets, including contemporary household appliances, were installed, while the original terrazzo floor and Art Deco cooker hood were preserved. In the bathrooms, appliances were placed on top of wooden floorboards, ensuring that the modifications remain easily reversible.

The garden has been restored to its original functional divisions: meadow, orchard, and vegetable garden. The topography has been carefully reinstated, with flagstones replaced in their original positions, maintaining the same wide, irregular joints that allow for the growth of short vegetation. To minimise maintenance needs, these joints have been filled with a lean substrate mixture that supports extensive perennial planting. Vegetation is kept short in high-traffic areas and allowed to grow longer in less frequently walked paths, creating soft borders between the flagstones and the adjacent flower beds. The unpaved paths are composed of lime-stabilised clay, closely matching the colour of the facing bricks of the house.

In the orchard, there are twenty-seven low-stemmed trained trees, featuring native pear and apple varieties. These species have been selected for their diversity, with multiple trees of each type to promote effective pollination, ensuring ripe fruit is available throughout the year. Additionally, there is a walnut tree, along with low- and half-stemmed cherry and plum trees of native varieties. Along the boundaries between the various areas – such as the orchard, vegetable garden, flower beds, and herb garden – low-trained fruit bushes (berries) have been planted.

The vegetable garden is both functional and organic, distinctly characterised by its different colours and overall appearance compared to the orchard. The boundary between the two areas aligns with the garden walls. The shape and layout of the vegetable garden adapt to the needs of the plants and the preferences of the users.

The slopes of the clay terrace edges on the meadow side transition between the house and garden, featuring flower beds that showcase a diverse array of shapes, flowering seasons, and colours. In the meadow, both old and new trees and shrubs reflect the area's original character. A young ginkgo, brought by the owners from Weimar, stands as a symbol of the connection between Weimar and Tervuren.

At the time of purchase, four of the five original trained linden trees – symbolising the five children – remained on the street side. The missing linden tree was replaced during the restoration. Originally, there were also trained pin oaks that provided shade for the large terrace and the studio windows; these too have been replaced.

The house and garden are becoming a home for art as well. The owners are thoughtfully identifying the ideal locations to showcase pieces from their collection of contemporary art and crafts, particularly favouring works from the CoBrA movement, along with glassware and photography. The furnishings and art objects are meticulously curated, selected gradually and in a 'glocal' and 'piecemeal' manner, to enhance the 'global' cohesion and composition of the space.

A complete restoration takes time. Work on the house commenced in August 2019 and received official approval in January 2022, a span of twenty-nine months. However, true completion is only realised when the 'law of help' is in effect, which has been the case since early 2024. Is the basement remaining dry? Are the façades, windows, and drainage systems holding up against heavy driving rain? How does the house perform in both summer and winter? Are the control mechanisms of the heating system functioning correctly?

After the completion of the work, with guarantees under pressure, there is a marked tendency to overreact if any issues arise. The meticulousness of the restoration, the piecemeal engineering approach, and the glocal perspective are all put to the test during these times. Maintaining composure is crucial to ensure that interventions remain focused and measured.

The restoration of the garden, from the repair of the topography to a state of incipient maturity, took nearly three years. It will take another three years for the new tall-stemmed trees to become established and for the overall landscape to take shape. By then, it will be 2027 – seventy years since Henry van de Velde's death and 100 years since the establishment of ENSAV–La Cambre,[62] which prompted his return to Belgium and the construction of La Nouvelle Maison.

[62] The École Nationale Supérieure des Arts Visuels (ENSAV) is often referred to simply as La Cambre, because it is located in the Abbey of La Cambre.

FACTS ABOUT LA NOUVELLE MAISON

Year of construction: 1928

Initial partial preservation order: 9 November 1994

Final full preservation order: 11 March 2024

Measured land area: 2,071.25 m^2

Total gross floor area: 458.44 m^2
- basement: 159.09 m^2
- ground storey: 158.49 m^2
- first storey: 140.86 m^2

Net usable living area: 256.97 m^2
- ground storey: 135.48 m^2
- first storey: 121.49 m^2

Net usable volume: 1,600.93 m^3

Restoration – building:
- Start date: August 2019
- Provisional acceptance: January 2022

Restoration – garden:
- Start date: April 2020
- End date: April 2023

Energy, heating, and hot water:
- Energy source: gas
- Annual consumption (July 2022 – July 2024): 110 kWh/m^2/year

PARTNERS IN THE RESTORATION

Clients and owners: Birgit and Thomas Rabe, Berlin

Supervisory heritage authority: Flemish Government – Agency for Immovable Heritage, Leuven

General construction contract: Renotec nv, Geel

General contract garden: elm landscaping, Kapelle-op-den-bos (Jo Groven)

Restoration architect: Arsis bv, Brussels (Guido Stegen, architect)

Safety coordination: Atelier 348, Kraainem (Pierre Ramon, architect)

Preliminary investigations:

Coordination: Arsis bv, Brussels (Guido Stegen, architect)

Building history research: JV architect bv, Harelbeke (Jérémy Vansteenkiste, architect)

Survey plans: Arsis bv, Brussels (Guido Stegen, architect)

Advice on historical garden: Ann Voets, Halle

Survey of land and underground infrastructures: Buro Van Eyken, Zemst

Stratigraphic research: Fenikx bv, Gentbrugge (Ann Verdonck, Marjolein Deceuninck)

Comfort analysis and energy audit: Buildwise nv, Brussels

Airtightness and thermography: BlowerTechnic bv, Mortsel

The House after Completion

COLSON WHITEHEAD CROOK MANIFESTO
HARLEM SHUFFLE
COLSON WHITEHEAD
THE UNDERGROUND RAILROAD COLSON WHITEHEAD
Nick Clegg Politics
COLSON WHITEHEAD The NICKEL BOYS
THE NEW CHINA PLAYBOOK

THE POWER BROKER
DICTATOR

Robert Seethaler
Das Café ohne Namen

歡迎
一九六二

HENRY VAN DE VELDE

Biography

3 April 1863
Henry van de Velde is born in Antwerp as the second youngest of eight children. His father is Guillaume van de Velde (1825–1901), a pharmacist from Brussels. His mother, Jeanne de Paepe (1826–88) from Ghent, comes from a long line of pharmacists, lawyers, and sailors. As a teenager, he aspires to become a conductor and composer. Music and theatre remain a major focus throughout his life.

1880–82
In 1880, van de Velde enrols at the Academy of Fine Arts in Antwerp. In 1882, he is introduced to works by Édouard Manet for the first time and is drawn to Impressionist art.

1886
He designs the cover for Max Elskamp's privately printed book of poems *L'Éventail japonais*, his first venture into the field of book design.

1887
At the IVth annual exhibition of the Les XX group in Brussels, Henry van de Velde encounters works by Georges Seurat and enthusiastically embraces Neo-Impressionism.

1888
Van de Velde joins the avant-garde group Les XX and subsequently participates in a number of exhibitions. Following his mother's death in July, he sinks into a severe depression. During this period, he embarks on an in-depth study of sociological and philosophical topics and later establishes personal connections with prominent French and Belgian anarchists and socialists.

1890–92
He designs embroideries and tapestries while also working as a typographer, creating fascinating abstract compositions in his drawings and woodcuts. He delivers lectures and publishes his ideas in articles. In 1892, he abandons painting for good.

1894
On 25 April, Henry van de Velde marries Marie-Louise (Maria) Sèthe (1867–1943), the daughter of a German-descended family. Her father, Gérard Sèthe (1827–93), was a textile entrepreneur in Paris and Brussels. That same year, van de Velde begins using the title 'Entrepreneur' on his letterhead, operating at his mother-in-law's address: 'ARTS D'INDUSTRIE & D'ORNEMENTATION. 62, DIEWEG, UCCLE-CALEVOET (PRÈS BRUXELLES)'.

1895
With financial support from his mother-in-law Louise Sèthe (1847–1923), who was born in Wiesbaden, the self-taught architect constructs his first house, Bloemenwerf, in the Brussels suburb of Uccle.
In the spring, art critic Julius Meier-Graefe (1867–1935) takes notice of Henry van de Velde. He introduces him to Siegfried Bing (1838–1905), a dealer of Japanese art who is preparing to open his gallery, L'Art Nouveau, in Paris. The three rooms designed by van de Velde displayed there at the end of 1895 spark a sensation, earning the Belgian designer instant fame.

1897
Collaborations with Meier-Graefe, Berlin painter Curt Herrmann (1854–1929), entrepreneur Eberhard von Bodenhausen (1868–1918), and art patron Harry Graf Kessler (1867–1937), among others, lead to van de Velde's first German commissions alongside numerous projects in Brussels and Paris.
On 13 March, his daughter Cornélie (Nele) van de Velde is born.
Starting in May, the rooms exhibited at Bing's gallery are presented in Dresden, boosting van de Velde's popularity in Germany.

1898
In Berlin, Henry van de Velde designs interiors and furniture for the gallery of Paul and Bruno Cassirer as well as the Keller & Reiner gallery. He and his circle of friends in Berlin decide to establish a limited liability company to support his work. This initiative quickly materialises with a capital of 130,000 marks.

1899
On 6 August, his daughter Hélène (nicknamed 'Puppie') is born. In Berlin, van de Velde redesigns the cigar shop of the Havana Compagnie, receiving great acclaim for its elegant furniture and innovative interior design. At an exhibition of the Munich Secession, he presents a luxurious study room, gaining additional clients. At the end of the year, the Paris gallery La Maison Moderne, which he designed for Julius Meier-Graefe, officially opens.

1900
Despite a wealth of commissions, Henry van de Velde finds himself unable to offset the financial losses of the van de Velde GmbH. Consequently, Bodenhausen sells the company to Berlin art dealer Hermann Hirschwald (1849–1906), who hires van de Velde in October with a substantial monthly salary of 1,000 marks. That autumn, van de Velde and his family relocate to Berlin. The same year, he receives a commission to redesign the salon of celebrity hairdresser François Haby (1861–1938). The project garners significant press acclaim in Berlin, further enhancing van de Velde's reputation.

1901
In the spring, a conflict arises with Hermann Hirschwald, who does not fully respect van de Velde's working methods. The contract is dissolved in November. By this time, van de Velde is a designer of European fame but finds himself completely destitute again. On 13 December, his third daughter, Anne, is born in Berlin. After many discussions, Harry Graf Kessler, together with Elisabeth Förster-Nietzsche (1846–1935), manages to arrange for van de Velde to be appointed as an advisor to Grand Duke Wilhelm Ernst of Saxe-Weimar-Eisenach for the applied arts and trades on 21 December.

1902
In the spring, van de Velde moves with his family to Weimar. His first commission from Elisabeth Förster-Nietzsche is the renovation and expansion of the Nietzsche Archive. At the same time, textile industrialist Herbert Eugen Esche (1874–1962) commissions him to build a villa in Chemnitz. On 9 July, the Museum Folkwang opens in Hagen, Westphalia, after van de Velde had spent two years renovating and refitting it at the request of Karl Ernst Osthaus (1874–1921). He also receives many new commissions, but being perceived as a 'star' leaves him feeling misunderstood and uncertain.

1904
Van de Velde, who had repeatedly pushed for the construction of the promised Kunstgewerbeschule (School of Applied Arts) in Weimar since 1903, is initially commissioned with the first phase of constructing this new arts school. On 13 March, twins Thylberte (Thylla) (1904–55) and Thylbert (Thyl) van de Velde (1904–80) are born.

1905
After several submissions, the construction of the School of Applied Arts is approved. The construction work is carried out in two phases and is completed in the autumn of 1906.

1908
In the spring, he and his family move into the house Hohe Pappeln in Weimar-Ehringsdorf. In March, van de Velde receives a new employment contract but remains a private employee of the Grand Duke. The School of Applied Arts does not become an institution of the state of Thuringia until 1919, under Walter Gropius, as the Staatliches Bauhaus Weimar.

1914
Van de Velde is inundated with commissions and, due to frequent travel, can only spend short periods in Weimar. The attacks and intrigues against him, ongoing since 1910, lead to a covert search for his successor.
Following the opening of his Werkbund Theatre in Cologne, he submits his resignation in Weimar on 25 July.
After the outbreak of the First World War on 1 August, the artist, now regarded as an 'enemy alien', faces further harassment.

1915
In April, he suggests August Endell (1871–1935), Hermann Obrist (1862–1927), and Walter Gropius (1883–1969) as candidates to succeed him.

1917
With the help of influential supporters, he manages to leave Germany for Switzerland on 10 April 1917. His daughter Nele follows in the spring of 1918, while the rest of the family is forced to remain in Germany.
Initially inactive in Bern, he soon establishes numerous connections with artists, writers, and pacifists from across Europe. In early summer, he meets Ernst Ludwig Kirchner (1880–1938) several times in Davos, supports the severely ill German Expressionist, and is portrayed by him in two striking woodcuts.

1918/19
In March 1918, van de Velde begins considering a fresh start in Uttwil on Lake Constance. There, he discovers the lakeside Haus am See, plans to rent it, and hopes to establish an artists' colony. Using his last remaining personal funds, he manages to purchase the house shortly before his family arrives at the end of 1918. Over time, several friends settle in Uttwil. Although van de Velde describes this period as a happy time, he himself remains unproductive and struggles to put down roots.
On 31 July 1919, his assets in Weimar, including the proceeds from the sale of the Hohe Pappeln house and other possessions, are confiscated.
On 25 October 1919, he meets Anton Kröller (1862–1941), a merchant and shipowner, in The Hague for the first time. Kröller and his German wife, Helene Kröller-Müller (1869–1939), plan to build a museum to house their unique modern art collection. Van de Velde is given a temporary contract with an annual salary of 20,000 guilders.

1920–25
At the beginning of 1920, van de Velde designs four prefabricated house types. He chooses the largest type, 'Haag', for himself and names his third personal home near Wassenaar, completed in the summer of 1921, De Tent (The Tent), as a reference to his temporary residence in the Netherlands.
Since 1922, influential friends in Belgium have been working to help him resuscitate his career in his native country.
In the spring of 1923, his monumental plans for the Kröller-Müller Museum are abandoned due to a lack of funding.

1926
Henry van de Velde's long-time friend Camille Huysmans (1871–1968), a publicist and leader of the socialists, repeatedly appeals to King Albert I in his capacity as Minister of Culture to facilitate van de Velde's return to Belgium. In a letter dated 2 March, the monarch agrees to this request and at the same time endorses Huysmans's proposal to establish a new design school in Brussels. Van de Velde's enemies launch a monthslong smear campaign in the press against his appointment as a professor in Ghent, and particularly against the founding of his new school.

1927
Over the course of the year, van de Velde establishes the Institut Supérieur des Arts Décoratifs (ISAD) in the abandoned abbey of La Cambre in Brussels and appoints its faculty. Alongside instruction in applied and fine arts, La Cambre will also offer courses in architecture, urban planning, stage design, choreography, fashion design, typography, and commercial graphics. In Tervuren, near Brussels, he builds his fourth and final home, La Nouvelle Maison. He moves into the house in 1928 with his wife and eldest daughter, Nele.

1929
For the Heinemann Foundation, which, according to its charter, supports elderly Jewish women, van de Velde designs a monumental retirement home complex with furnishings in Hanover. This architectural commission, his final one in Germany, is completed in 1931.

1933
In recognition of his 70th birthday on April 3, 1933, the Belgian government commissions him to design the University Library in Ghent.
On April 15, 1933, he is appointed as the artistic advisor to the National Railway Company of Belgium (SNCFB). In the following years, he designs new locomotives as well as the railcar interiors. The logo he created for the SNCFB at that time is still in use today.

1936
The Dutch government commissions him to design a 'temporary' building for the now-nationalised Kröller-Müller Museum in Otterlo. The foundation stone is laid on 18 May 1937, and the museum opens on July 13, 1938. The museum is later expanded two more times in accordance with his plans, in 1941–44 and again in 1953–57.
On August 1, he is granted emeritus status at the University of Ghent. At the same time, he resigns from his position as director of the La Cambre design school. In the same year, he is tasked with the planning of the Belgian Pavilion for the 1937 Paris Expo.

1938
The Belgian state commissions the now 75-year-old van de Velde once again to design the Belgian Pavilion for the 1939 New York Expo, which he has prefabricated in Belgium. During the opening in May 1939, van de Velde is made an honorary citizen of New York.

1939–1944
In 1939, van de Velde is appointed a member of the Royal Commission on Monuments and Landscapes, where he reviews and revises thousands of building applications. After the German invasion of Belgium, the German military administration confirms him in this office, which he holds until the end of the German occupation of Belgium in 1944.

1945/46
After the end of the war, his opponents become more vocal, accusing van de Velde of collaborating with the enemy.
He is required to answer to the judicial authorities; however, the proceedings are quickly terminated.

1947–1953
In the late summer of 1947, van de Velde moves to Oberägeri, near Zurich, with his daughter Nele. The last years of his life are dedicated to writing his memoir Story of My Life. The book is published in a shortened version in German in 1962.
His last trip by aeroplane to the Netherlands in 1953 is for overseeing his plans for the expansion of the Kröller-Müller Museum in Otterlo.

25 October 1957
After a brief illness, Henry van de Velde passes away in a Zurich hospital at the age of 95 due to complications of the flu. His ashes are buried next to his wife's grave at the cemetery in Tervuren, near Brussels.

1st edition 2025

produktsicherheit@penguinrandomhouse.de
(The above information is mandatory information according to GPSR and should be used for all queries relating to the safety of our books)

A CIP catalogue record for this book is available from the British Library.
Library of Congress Control Number: 2025940483

Editorial direction Prestel: Katharina Haderer, Markus Eisen
Copyediting: Sylee Gore
Design and layout: Justus Oehler, Pentagram Design
Production management: Cilly Klotz
Separations: LUDWIG:media gmbh
Printing and binding: Longo SPA|AG, Bolzano
Typeface: Degular, Baskerville, Futura, Courier
Paper: 170 g/qm Galaxi Supermatt, 115 g/qm Munken Print White

MIX Paper | Supporting responsible forestry FSC® C023164

Penguin Random House Verlagsgruppe FSC® N001967

Printed in Italy

ISBN 978-3-7913-7898-5

www.prestel.com

Image Credits
t top, b bottom, r right, l left, c center

Florian Holzherr: pp. 4/5, 8/9, 11, 12, 13, 32/33, 35 tl, 37 tr, 37 br, 37 crt, 37 crb, 39 tl, 39 cc, 39 bc, 39 tl, 39 cl, 39 bl, 41br, 43 tl, 43 tcl, 43 tcr, 43 tr, 43 cl, 43 cr, 45 tr, 45 bc, 47 tl, 47 br, 48, 49, 50 b, 53 cblb, 53 ctl, 53 bl, 53 bcl, 53 bc, 53 bcr, 53 br, 62, 63 tl, 63 cr, 71 tcl, 71 tcr, 71 tr, 71 c, 71 cr, 71 bc, 71 br, 73 tc, 73 ctl, 73 ctl, 73 bl, 75, 77bl, 80 tc, 80 cc, 80 cclt, 80 cr, 81 tl, 81 tcl, 81 tcr, 81 cl, 81 ccl, 81 cc, 81 ccr, 81 bl, 83 tr, 83 cr, 83 bl, 83 bcl, 83 br, 88/89, 90/91, 92, 92/93, 94, 95, 96, 97, 98/99, 100, 101, 102, 103, 104/105, 106, 107 b, 108, 109, 110, 111, 112, 113, 114, 115, 116, 117, 118, 119, 120, 121, 122, 123, 124, 125, 126, 127, 128, 129, 130, 131, 132, 133, 134, 135, 136, 137, Cover

Arsis bv – Guido Stegen: pp. 35 b, 39 tc, 41 tr, 41 bl, 41 bc, 43 b, 44, 45 tl, 50 t, 53 tl, 53 tcl, 53tcc, 53 tcr, 53 tr, 53 ctcl, 53 ctc, 53 ctcr, 53 ctr, 53 cbl, 53 cbcl, 53 cbc, 53 cbcr, 53 cbtr, 63 tc, 63 tr, 63 ctl, 63 cbc, 63 bl, 63 br, 64, 65, 66, 68, 70, 71 tl, 71 cl, 71 bl, 73 tl, 73 tr, 73 cbl, 73 ccl, 73 ctcr, 73 cbcr, 73 cr, 73 bcl, 73 cbr, 73 cr, 76, 77 tl, 77 tr, 77 cl, 77 c, 77 cr, 77 br, 79 tr, 79 cr, 79 bl, 79 bc, 79 br, 80 tl, 80 tcl, 80 tcr, 80 cl, 80 cclt, 80 cclb, 80 ccbr, 80 bl, 80 bcl, 80 bcr, 80 br, 81 tr, 81 cr, 81 bc, 81 br, 83 tl, 83 tc, 83 cl, 83 bcr

Thomas Föhl: pp. 19 t, 19 br

© Birger Stichelbaut: pp. 95, 107 t

Bridgeman Images: pp. 24, 37 bl

CIVA Collections, Brussels: pp. 17, 25 t, 39 bl

Dépôt de la Bibliothèque Royale aux AML, Bruxelles (Belgique): pp. 25 b, 27 tl, 27 tr, 27br, 30, 31, 37 tl, 45 bl, 45 br

ENSAV - La Cambre, Bruxelles, inv. S 1002 © Henry van de Velde Foundation (Pays-Bas). Photo Guido Stegen: pp. 40, 40/41, 46/47, 47tr, 55, 56, 57, 58, 59, 60, 60/61, 61, 79 tl, 79 cl

Leon Ploegaerts and Pierre Puttemans, Atelier L'oeuvre architecturale de Henry van de Velde, Brussels 1987, p. 24: p. 35 tr

Private Collection, © Hers Family: p. 69

Public Domain: p. 19 bl

Thomas Rabe: p. 10

Universiteitsarchief KU Leuven. Archief Raphaël Verwilghen. Fotoalbum 10: pp. 26, 27 bl